BITS AND PIECES OF A COUNTRY

Fidel Nwobi

Copyright © 2020 by Fidel Nwobi

All rights reserved. No part of this publication may be reproduced, stored in any form of retrieval system or transmitted in any form or by any means without prior permission in writing from the publishers except for the use of brief quotations in a book review.

Dedication

To Regina Chinwendu Nwobi:
My wife, friend and confidant.

CONTENTS

Chapter 1. Oily Land 5

Chapter 2. Sister Mabel 43

Chapter 3. Landslide Victory 68

Chapter 4. Go Slow 117

Chapter 5. Entry Restricted 160

Chapter 6. Particular Wahala 196

Chapter 7. Flying Colours 237

Chapter 8. Eleven Seventeen 262

CHAPTER 1.
OILY LAND

It is the twenty-first century. Several years had gone by since the much-awaited new millennium rolled in. Successive Nigerian governments had previously assigned some magical powers to this century. Nigerians had been witnesses to such wishful proclamations called policy thrusts and development plans. Health for all by the year 2000; houses for all by the year 2000; food for all by the year 2000; education for all by the year 2000. There had been so much hope built around the year 2000 that the citizens prayed to deities and expected the coming of Utopia in Nigeria. The year 2000 was pre-decorated with garlands as a wonder year; a year of inexplicable turnaround in the lives of many Nigerians like Egonakpari and Uyaemena, his wife. Egonakpari and his immediate family lived far away from the central seat of power. Aso Rock, Nigeria's federal seat of power was some seven hundred kilometres away from Egonakpari's home in Adagalaba, an oil-producing community in the lower Niger Delta flood plain. Ironically, over ninety percent of the money with which Aso Rock was built and was currently being run came from Adagalaba and her sister communities in the Niger Delta.

Egonakpari was ignorant of the details outlined above. He was recognized by the oil exploration and production company operating in his family land. Niger Oil listed Egonakpari as one of their landlords. As a landlord, he was offered a "contract appointment". Contract appointment is a contrivance by employers of labour in Nigeria. It is designed to rob the employee of most of his supposed rights as a worker. In the package of a contracted staff member, the company is under no obligation to provide the employee with any form of medical allowance, housing allowance, or transportation allowance. Employees in this category are easily laid off without severance packages. They cannot protest. They have no right to embark on industrial action. In fact, they have no direct contract with Niger Oil. A contractor to Niger Oil is the bona fide employer of contract staff. The contractor only seconds such a staff member to Niger Oil.

Moreover, the job scope of a contract staff member is not always defined. He is forced to guzzle down every cup of bitter-sweet concussion offered to him. Otherwise, he'd lose out entirely. After all, oil companies in Nigeria are very precious to the Federal Government of Nigeria. They are priceless, and their interests are uniquely prized above the lives and well-being of the very citizens of Nigeria. Officers and men of the Mobile Police Force, the official symbol of government brutality, are always there to remind any "stubborn" landlord that might is right. Egonakpari had learnt early enough not to appear confrontational to oil companies. He was an eyewitness to the killing of his four uncles for daring to challenge this same oil company. He always reasoned that he had a wife and three young children. He considered it would be foolish and untimely to die at that time, making his wife a widow and his children fatherless. It was his considered opinion that a bird in the hand is worth two in the bush. He, therefore, chose to be considered foolish and cowardly for the sake of the well-being of his immediate family.

"Akpa!" a voice called. Egonakpari heard his name and immediately recognised the voice of the caller. Only his friend and colleague, Ogadimma, could call him so.

"Ogadi!" he responded without moving, not even turning his head. "Is it raining yet?" That was a veiled way of asking if salaries had been paid.

"Akpa, rain or no rain, I am sick and tired of all these. When will God remember me and my family?"

"How do you mean?"

"Is this forest rich enough for a dog to catch game?" he asked in reference to the fulfilment or otherwise of the job each of them was doing for a living.

"What is better than working for an oil company?" Egonakpari asked.

"Don't be silly! Do you really think you are working with an oil company?"

"But where are you? Is this not Niger Oil?" Egonakpari insisted.

Ogadi nodded his head in mock affirmation. Then he added voice to it, saying "This is Niger Oil, the foremost oil-producing company in Nigeria. There's no doubt about that. This is Niger Oil, indeed! Hey, listen! Have you ever heard about the hand of Esau and the voice of Jacob? This is exactly what I see here. Don't be deceived into thinking you are working with an oil company. You work for Chief Akudinogwu. You are a little higher than his personal slave. He collects money for the work you do, and then pays you peanuts."

"My question remains unanswered: *rain don fall?*" Egonakpari persisted.

"Well, they have paid. Chief Akudinogwu was here this morning for that purpose," Ogadi answered. "What I am seriously contemplating is quitting this God-forsaken job and take my destiny in my own hands."

"What exactly do you intend to do?"

"Buying and selling, of course. We all know that the most lucrative engagements here are illegal oil bunkering, holding a political office, or executing contracts for oil firms or the government. But we equally know that those businesses are for those fortunate ones whose gods fished for them and equally de-boned the fishes, serving them fat flesh on a platter. They are, for Nigerians, well-connected to the corridors of power. Buying and selling shall pay me better than this slave labour I do here in the name of a job."

"I admire your courage to navigate the troubled economic waters of Nigeria."

"I know it is a high-risk venture to do this. All the same, my mind is already made up."

"I'd better pick up my envelope immediately. My creditors are already harassing me daily. Clinton's school fees must be paid also."

Egonakpari rode his bicycle to the location. There, he signed the necessary documents and received his salary which was enclosed in a brown envelope. He was given a big portfolio, big only in nomenclature. Being called a Supervisor, Surveillance and Environmental Department, was only a terminology for a security man cum manual labourer whose operational area is a specified stretch of oil and gas pipeline. It was his duty to keep close watch over a ten-kilometre stretch of pipeline. Wilful destruction of pipelines by vandals had become a common and often recurring crime, not only in the Niger Delta region but throughout oil pipelines across the country. Oil firms now take on the extra responsibility of patrolling pipelines within a ten-kilometre radius of their operational bases. The Department of Petroleum Resources is responsible for the safety of pipelines outside the scope of the oil companies.

In addition to this surveillance job, it was Egonakpari's responsibility to clear bushes sprouting up along this stretch, and to carry out any other duty that might be assigned to him. Day and night, he would use his bicycle to go through this stretch. Armed with a walkie-talkie, a torch, and a machete, he'd signal the head of the security department whenever he sensed some infringement on his official domain. Part of the land on which those pipes were laid belonged to Egonakpari's family. By sheer force through the Land Use Act of 1976, the Federal Government stripped ownership of those lands from the original owners. In theory, Egonakpari and some of his family folks still laid claim to ownership of the land, but in practice, they neither owned the land nor enjoyed the resources deposited there by Mother Nature.

Before Egonakpari left the house that morning, he had a dose of troubles from his family. His first child, Clinton, woke up with nothing but his school fees in mind. Without greeting his parents with a "good morning", he demanded his school fees from his father. Clinton was nine years old. "Have you greeted me this morning?" Egonakpari asked him. "Or is that what your teacher teaches you?"

"Erm, good morning, Papa, but I was waiting for you last night to come home. You didn't come until I fell asleep."

"Ah! So, how did I contribute to your falling asleep without seeing me?"

"But Papa, Teacher Smart talked about sending us back from school in the next two days if we do not pay our school fees. I don't want to be sent out of school."

"Don't worry, my son. Your school fees will be paid. You will not be sent out."

"Papa, do you intend to see Teacher Smart about this?"

"There'll be no need for that. You'll pay your school fees."

"No, Papa, this time I would be worried. That's what you have always said. In the end, I usually end up being sent away from school."

"Do you advise I steal to pay your school fees?"

"No, Papa! But the office! You may get money from the office. Is it not from there that you usually get money?"

"My salary has not been paid. Once it is paid, your fees will be paid."

"But Papa, when are they paying your salary? They ought to know that you'll pay my school fees."

"You ask too many questions, Clinton. You have not done anything this morning. Or do you still consider yourself a baby?"

"Nnabuenyi and Obumneke are still sleeping. I cannot sweep the house and make the bed while they are lying down."

"How often do you need this correction? You could always start with washing the dishes. Wash your face, brush your teeth, and empty your bowels if you choose to. Tackle such things as you can do first. Before you are through with them, the younger ones will be up. Then you can sweep the house and make the bed."

While the duo was talking, Uyaemena was busy making the fire to warm the *nsala* soup that was left over from the previous day. She intended that Clinton and Nnabuenyi would take cassava *fufu* with that *nsala* soup for breakfast. Nnabuenyi, Egonakpari's second child, was four years old. Obumneke, the only girl child in the family, was a baby, barely nine months old. Her staple foods were *pap* made from local maize and breast milk. While Uyaemena administered the kitchen, ensuring that every loose end from that angle was tidied up, Egonakpari was busy releasing their home-raised fowls and goats from the pen.

The pen and the kitchen were twin detached houses. Both were bamboo-reinforced, mud-walled, and thatch-roofed. Both were about ten meters away from the main house, and three meters from each other. The main house was a contraption that displayed some modernism on the facade. The walls were mud-based and reinforced with bamboo. The local masons who raised the structure exhibited some high sense of ingenuity as the walls were symmetrically built. The outer walls were overlaid with cement, giving it the modern finishing face it wore. The roof was of corrugated iron sheets. Pieces of local raffia mat were horizontally suspended beneath the wooden skeleton of the roof, just above the head of any six-footer. This served as a ceiling, primarily for temperature control.

That main house was a two-bedroom apartment. A single entrance led into the sitting room. It had two other doors connecting each bedroom to the sitting room. It had no bathroom or lavatory facilities. The furniture in the sitting room consisted of two benches, each five feet long, a locally fabricated collapsible chair, a centre table made of cane wood, and two smaller tables, each placed in a corner of the sitting room. The first table supported a battery-powered radio/cassette recorder. Atop the second table was a 14-inch Sharp colour television. The television served more as decoration than for information and entertainment. This was so because that part of Adagalaba had neither a power supply from the national grid nor from the gas turbine built by Niger Oil for its operations. Rural folks were not happy that the oil company had violated the terms of the memorandum of understanding reached between both parties four years earlier.

That agreement included the provision of free electricity, construction of a total of ten kilometres of rural road network, employing twenty young men in low cadre positions and four in executive positions, and reserving ten percent of the contracts awarded by the oil firm to contractors indigenous to Adagalaba. It was spelt out that all these must be achieved within four years. However, only two kilometres of road had been built. Ten young men had been employed as contract staff. No personnel had been placed in an executive position. The community was as much in darkness as it had been from the beginning.

The knotty issues contained in that memorandum of understanding were the remote causes that led to the death of Egonakpari's four uncles. Those men had championed the cause of the community, insisting that Niger Oil would not continue to drill oil from their land, with the attendant hazard of oil spillage and other forms of negative environmental impact associated with oil-drilling activities, without adequately compensating the community. They led others to shut down facilities of the oil firm in Adagalaba, insisting that Niger Oil would only operate in that community on the condition that they draw up and ultimately sign such a memorandum of understanding with the community.

Within twenty-four hours of that action, a combined team of soldiers and mobile policemen were drafted to the scene with a 'shoot at sight' order from the state Governor. Under the protection of the military boys, Niger Oil resumed operations. Community folks were warned to stay clear of the operational and residential areas of the oil firm, or risk being shot. When the community stakeholders met and reviewed the situation, they agreed to embark on a peaceful protest march. Their aim was to march to the gate of the premises housing the oil firm, register their displeasure, and seek audience with the firm's Community Relations Officer. When they got close to that entrance, however, the military boys opened fire on them and felled twenty-four men, including the four prominent uncles of Egonakpari.

That shooting caused a major crisis in the community. Neither Niger Oil workers nor the villagers enjoyed peace for a fortnight following that shooting. While youths from Adagalaba engaged in guerrilla-style warfare, sabotaging the interest of Niger oil, the oil firm, through the mobile policemen guarding their installations and personnel, bared its fangs. The military men were at liberty to display all the beastly instinct in them. They ravaged village women, with or without their consent, married or unmarried. Men were subjected to very degrading treatment. It did not matter if the man was an unruly youth or a respectable grandfather. All that mattered was that they were indigenes of Adagalaba.

Like athletes positioned on their marks and ready to go, Egonakpari and Clinton set off for the river at the same time. They set their faces towards one of the waterfronts on the River Niger. Ikposinemem, their dog, who had been lying idly, immediately jumped up and followed her masters. She seemed to have been waiting for that moment. This October, the Niger had begun to overflow its banks. Besides human, domestic and industrial waste wilfully deposited into the river by men, the river was acquiring more of these deposits by reason of its tendency to extend its territory. The footpath leading to the waterfront had become a gully, the result of centuries of the combined assault of human feet and the vagaries of weather.

As father, son, and Ikposinemem the dog made their descent, meandering along that ancient footpath, the humans used their hands to ward off leaves of elephant grass which seemed to engage their kin from the other part of the footpath in a handshake. Those leaves had acquired enough reservoir of water between the previous night and this morning, and they were generous enough to donate some of the water in drops to the bodies of these early intruders. The rather cold morning notwithstanding, father, son, and dog continued their downward movement to the river. Just before they arrived at the waterfront, Egonakpari went behind a nearby bush and emptied his bowels. When he re-joined his son, the dog remained behind to do some justice to part of that waste.

That waterfront was well-prepared to serve the needs of the community. As they approached, there was an improvised hanger for garments. On this, father and son hung their garments and dived into the river. From one part of the waterfront, the boy swam to some distance, buried his frame in the water, and drank his fill of water. At another part, the father busied himself with his routine daily personal hygiene programme. He washed himself thoroughly, ensuring that no trace of dirt or faeces remained visible on his body. Ikposinemem was busy, roaming the forest in search of her own pleasure. Back at the house, Clinton was disappointed that it was the same old diet of cassava and *nsala* soup for breakfast, and he expressly told his parents so.

"Don't we ever change our diet in this house?" he asked.

"Would you shut up and eat your food?" his father corrected. "Shouldn't you be expressing appreciation to God that there is some food in this house?"

"What has this little boy done?" his mother asked, defending him. "Does he not have any right to express his preferences and desires?"

"Uyaemena, mind your language!" Egonakpari warned his wife. "So, you are the one teaching him all these stubborn traits I've been noticing of late, eh?"

"Stubborn traits indeed! It's in the genes," Uyaemena fired back. "He inherited it from his father's lineage. If you were not ready to cater for a family, why raise one in the first place?"

"Mouth like a crayfish! The thing about you is that you are all bone and no flesh. If I touch you with my hands, you'll break in two."

"That's right!" she concurred. "I am all bone and no flesh because you have milked me dry in your house. Everyone knows I was very well-fed and good-looking before I left my father's house for this miserable house of yours."

"What does that imply, stinging tongue?"

"I presume you don't expect me to interpret that to you, your lordship?"

"I am running out of patience. Don't let me descend on you."

"How many wrestling contests have you won in your life? Go and engage in some more profitable things."

"What manner of profitable things, Mrs Know-all?"

"Go and get some money and let your family smile. We were not created to suffer."

"It's quite unfortunate that you don't appreciate my efforts in this home."

"No! It's rather unfortunate that you want your family to applaud your ineptitude. This is typical of the proverbial owl that farted and asked its kinsmen to clap for him. Well, they all snapped their fingers in disapproval, saying that mischief is never applauded."

Afterwards, she turned to her son, encouraging him to eat.

"Never mind, son, things shall get better soon."

The little boy felt some sense of victory. He therefore ate and left for school. That school was the only educational facility situated in this rainforest and swampy village called Adagalaba. Total physical infrastructure in the school consisted of two blocks: a block of four classrooms, and another block of two classrooms. Part of the second block was a large room with the inscription "STAFF ROOM". Added to this was a single-room security house at the entrance to the school, and the school lavatory, which was some forty meters away from the main block. These made up Adagalaba Primary School.

Both buildings bore signs of dilapidation. Several sections of walls were cracked, creating crevices used by lizards and geckoes for safe retreat purposes. Viewing that block from the exterior, the roof of the four-classroom block looked like a normal house roof. The immediate surroundings were overgrown virgin rainforest. An open door revealed the interior layout of one of the classrooms. There was only a desk in the classroom. That was for the class teacher. Clinton and other members of his class were seated on the bare clay floor. The lower parts of the walls looked like an abstract impression of confusion, courtesy of deliberate and unconscious posting and stains that had spanned over a decade. With this classroom, as with others in the school, the law governing the walls was: the higher you go, the cleaner it looks. However, the top manifested some huge holes on the corrugated iron sheets used as roofing material. The classroom did not have a ceiling. There was a blackboard, so to speak. In actual fact, it looked like a grey board.

The class teacher's chair was empty. He had gone to one of the classrooms to engage in local gossip with a female colleague. Pupils in his class had a field day, as always, chatting, fighting, and playing. Since their arrival this morning, the class teacher had only taken them for two lessons, arithmetic and primary science. As it approached one o'clock in the afternoon Nigerian time, the teacher, Mr Smart Akpati found his way into the classroom and ordered every pupil to stand. Complaints being lodged by a dozen children almost at the same time fell on deaf ears. Smart was immune to such a barrage of complaints. And these children, as a result of constant and repeated practice, had come to know that it was their apportioned lot neither to attract attention nor to get a response from the teacher at such times. However, Smart the teacher would be dead wrong to think that the children would stop.

Daily, therefore, they continued in the tradition that had evolved. No sooner had Teacher Smart come in than he hit the table three times with his clenched fist. On this signal, the children all stood up and greeted him in unison: *"Good afternoon, sir!"*

Almost simultaneously, the bells rang, assembling the entire school for closing formalities. Smart was right on target. "Children!" he began. "Tell your parents that no pupil shall be allowed into his or her class if he or she has not paid his or her school fees. Remind them to give you your Parent-Teacher Association levies also. Failure to bring your levies will translate to your not being allowed to sit the forthcoming examinations.

Now, pick up your bags and quietly leave for the assembly ground."

"Yes, sir!" the children chorused.

Following the brief address was a tumultuous scene created by every child's determined effort to leave the classroom before the others. Even Teacher Smart himself was in a hurry to leave. Soon, they all joined other children in front of the four-classroom block. There were six staff members employed in the school. This comprised of five teaching staff, including the Headteacher, and a security man. The assembly could not be held. Though the bells had been rung, a storm was gathering. On very short notice, the clouds let go their torrential rain, complementarily spiced with earth-brightening lightening and deafening sounds of thunder. Every child and teacher found their way back to their classroom.

The noise of rain drowned out every other noise in the classroom. Again, from practice, the children began to effectively adjust their positions. Several plastic bowls were being strategically positioned to contain the threats of raindrops disturbing the comfortable sitting positions of these little kids. The rain came with a fierce cold wind. In quick response to the threat of cold and dripping rainwater, the children crowded together, characteristic of day-old chicks in need of some warmth. Principally to keep warm and secondarily to fight the boredom of inactivity and hunger, Teacher Smart raised a song:

Akwukwo n'aso uso
Ma ona rahu n'ammuta
Onye were nkasiobi
Oga amuta akwukwo
Ma oburukwa na nne ya na nna ya nwere ego
Ma oburukwa na nne ya na nna ya nwere ego
Oga amuta akwukwo osiso!

That song was to remind every child of the importance of western education, and that education is not cheap. The entire class was emotionally involved in the song. With frenetic hand-clapping and feet-stamping accompanying the song, the class was totally oblivious to the abrupt stop of the rain. Hunger pangs and the eagerness to go home, which had always been the predominant emotions at such times as this, ironically seemed to have vanished now. Teacher Smart, who had been lulled to sleep by the songs, now started up. He looked at his wristwatch. "My goodness!" he spoke to himself. "It's already two o'clock."

One whole hour had passed, yet it only seemed to be like minutes. He hit the table with his fist three consecutive times. At that, you could have heard a pin drop.

"Hello, children!" Teacher Smart began. "It's time to go home. But before then, let us pray!"

All the children knelt. Then Smart said, "The Lord's prayer!"

The children recited:
Our father,
Who art in heaven,
Hallowed be thy name;
Thy kingdom come;
Thy will be done on earth;
As it is in heaven.
Give us this day
Our daily bread.
Forgive us our trespasses,
As we forgive those who trespass against us.
And lead us not into temptation;
But deliver us from all evil.
For thine is the kingdom,
The power and the glory,
For ever and ever, Amen!

As soon as that was over, they all knew that the next thing they had to do was to sing a song announcing that classes for the day were over and, at the same time, showing appreciation for their teacher. So, they sang:

Anyi agbasa go
Akwu-kwo

*Ekene diri
Nde nkuzi
Kuziri anyi
Akwukwo.*

As soon as closing formalities were over, Clinton dashed towards the school lavatory. Visiting the school lavatory was a daily routine for him on weekdays. The privilege of using a purpose-built latrine was a luxury he and his father's family could not afford in the house. There, everybody defecated in nearby bushes, in the various ponds scattered all over Adagalaba, or by the bank of the famous River Niger. While approaching the solitary latrine house, he could perceive the strong stench of the over-used pit latrine. Clinton pulled off his shirt and dropped it on the luxurious green lawn at the entrance to the lavatory.

As he opened the door, which was made of wood and corrugated iron sheets which had turned brown from rust, he was warmly welcomed by a swarm of big green flies and the unenviable assault of hot air that oozed out of the pit. Decomposing human faeces had reached a dangerous level in that pit. Soon it would overflow, like a carelessly filled cup of hot maize cereal. The lad closed the door again, removed his shorts, and found a place for them on the extreme left of the lavatory floor, quite safe from the horde of white maggots doing their macabre dance inside that pit and on the periphery of the hole.

Some of those poor little creatures seemed to dare him by crawling out of their chosen place. He moved forward, turned around to face the door again, spread his legs, and positioned himself in a comfortable squatting position. Then he felt a rumble in his lower abdomen. Done! Clinton stood up to discover that a member of the maggot family had acquired some new kind of effrontery to challenge his superiority. After all, he thought within himself, they lived on his waste products. The disrespectful little thing had blindly crawled very close to Clinton's shorts. The boy, now in a combative mood, reached for his shorts as a matter of priority. Next, he raised his right foot and let it descend on the little mass of flesh called a maggot. Not satisfied, he used that foot to crush the maggot out of any form of existence.

"Eh hen!" he said to himself. "I am sure no place is found for it on earth." It was after winning that battle that Clinton realized he had nothing to clean himself up. He could still feel the wet sticky substance that must have turned his anal region into a big mess. Then he heard a knock on the door.

"Who's there?" a voice asked.

"Yes?" Clinton answered.

"Are you finished?" the voice of a much bigger boy asked. "Don't you know that others are waiting?"

Clinton quickly opened the door and left the lavatory.

"Hm!" the other boy exclaimed, using his index finger and thumb to mockingly hold his nostrils. "What did you eat that smells like decomposing human flesh?"

"Nothing!" Clinton answered, frowning in disapproval of such interrogation.

"Are you frowning at me?" the boy asked and gave Clinton a knock on the head. "Next time, you'll learn how not to be disrespectful to your elders."

"Hmm! What have I done now? What have I done?" Clinton cried, and moved to the rear of the building. Here, he picked some green leaves, bent forward and cleaned himself up in his own style. Then he thought about the maggot he had just killed. He wondered why the maggot left its kith and kin to wander towards his garments. He tasked his mind to understand why those maggots loved human waste as much as they did. He remembered that their home-raised fowls and dogs also had a special love for human faeces.

He looked around him to make sure nobody could see him. Then he put his left hand behind him, navigated to the anus, and used his forefinger to scrub the anus. Then he quickly pulled out that hand and lifted it right to the tip of his nostrils. He smelled it again and again. He ruled that the odour was not as foul as everybody had made him believe it was. Just about everybody he knew treated human faeces as if it were the worst item on Planet Earth. Now, he knew it was not exactly as they always painted it in their everyday picture. After all, some human beings emitted odour worse than this, he thought within himself.

Clinton's school uniform, like those of most other pupils in Adagalaba Primary School, was now light brown in colour. Originally bright white, those shirts and blouses had lost the power of whiteness and rather settled for the more manageable brownish hue. In a way, this resultant colour perfectly blended with the deep brown colour of the boys' shorts and the girls' skirts. For Clinton, his shirt had very many stories to tell. It obviously had seen better days. It was in a state of permanent crease. This resulted from the fact that it never experienced a pressing iron. It, therefore, assumed the look of custom-creased woven fabric.

There were more button positions without buttons on that shirt than those with buttons. Clinton's shorts looked as brown as they had been from the beginning. The only noticeable change about that pair of shorts were the two holes of almost equal proportion diametrically positioned on either part of the buttocks. Otherwise, that pair of shorts was amazingly good.

On his way home, Clinton remembered there was a hurdle to cross. It was a task to wade through the flooded road that centrally served every resident of Adagalaba on that side of the divide. It was indeed a necessary but unpleasant hurdle. At the peak of the flooding season, that road was always impassable. Being a part of the lower Niger Delta, Adagalaba always received her fair share of flood-related problems. School attendance always dropped drastically when the flood menace reared its head.

Running almost parallel to this road, about one kilometre apart, was a well-elevated, solidly constructed road. This latter road had drainage facilities on both sides. The topmost part was overlaid with asphalt of about three-inch thickness. From the ramp on the Niger, this road led to the gas recycling plant of Niger Oil Ltd and continued until it terminated at the staff residential base.

Clinton wondered why that road serving Niger Oil was so good and so different from this one that served most of the community folks. That knowledge was too advanced for him. He wished the flooded road he was about to pass through could be exchanged for the other. He went through the rituals of removing all of his garments and made straight for the flooded way. Due to the rather high volume of rains that season, the Niger and some other rivulets and ponds were already overflowing their banks. He continued his homeward movement. Whenever he felt a kind of sensation, he'd put his hand into the water and pull a leech from his skin. Those creatures always had a way of receiving signals that a human was invading their home territory.

Every flooding season, Adagalaba Primary School loses nearly fifty percent of its pupil population. Clinton resolved that this evening, he'd ask his father pertinent questions about some apparent contradictions he saw around him. He wondered why his parents and most other natives lived in mud-walled houses with thatched roofs while those visitors who worked with Niger Oil lived in modern cement-block houses with oven-baked coloured aluminium roofing sheets. He could not understand why there was an uninterrupted electric power supply to those houses in the Niger Oil camp and base while his family and their community folks continued to make use of kerosene lanterns and candles.

He was amazed at the fact that Niger Oil workers seemed so highly favoured by God that God gave them good roads to their housing estate and workplace; that even at the peak of the rainy season, Niger Oil workers had unhindered access to their workplace and residential flats, yet some of the natives who owned the land were perennially sentenced to forced annual leave from their homes when the rains came. He was puzzled to note the everyday truth that so many motor vehicles were being used by Niger Oil workers while the majority of his people either moved on foot or managed to own bicycles. Only a few owned motorbikes, and an even more negligible few, like chief Akudinogwu, owned motor cars.

He was bewildered to observe that those who lived on the other divide seemed to own all the money in the land, buying the fishes and agricultural produce sold by his parents and other natives. Yet, it was a wonder that the natives never seemed to have enough money to pay their children's school fees. He could not comprehend why those Niger Oil workers never enrolled their children in the same school as the children of the natives. He also wondered why those people always looked happier, fresher, and better-fed than his own people.

Clinton was not very comfortable observing that they all seemed to live in the same community, yet there evidently existed a very wide gulf between the natives, so-called landlords, and the visitors working with Niger Oil. Adding to his confusion was the prevailing penchant for religion among his people, a penchant that was unequivocally lacking among Niger Oil workers.

He remembered the very first day he had the opportunity to follow his father to the base. There was

…le and sparkle of that office environment.
…s the almost perfect beauty of the recreated lush green grass lawns that adorned the landscape of that environment. There was the serenity-creating ambience occasioned by the beautiful arrangement of flowers and shade-giving trees, carefully planted in rows to further enhance the aesthetic look of that landscape. There was the cemented part of the floor area and the well laid out roads.

There was the cooling device he saw and felt in the office of a man his father referred to as "the manager". The cooling box-like contraption suspended on the wall was called an air-conditioner. There was the refreshment he felt as the cool breeze from this device gently touched his face, and meandered its way beyond his garment, and caressed his skin.

But then, there was the fascination of being that close to the gas flaring point of the gas plant. He saw the enormity of that flame that seemed to burn eternally like the hellfire the pastor of his local church always warned about. He resolved to also ask his father again to know why his father and his friends always discussed this fire in negative terms. They had often talked about that fire being one major source of environmental pollution; that the effect of the fire could shorten their lives, reduce crop yield on the farms, retard physical and mental development of human beings, stunt the growth of domestic and wild animals, and make their community less safe for human habitation. Yet, his father worked for Niger Oil, and Niger Oil workers and their families looked that good and enviable.

Clinton took the last step out of that brownish muddy pool. Then he made for the trunk of a fallen palm tree lying idly by the wayside. Standing on this tree trunk, he stooped low and scooped some water to clean up his legs. Dark strips of dirt and mud now dotted parts of his legs, from the waist downwards. As he walked home, he could hear the familiar chirping and singing of birds. Such sound was not strange to him. At the age of nine, he had already learnt how to set traps for birds. He had also shown appreciable skill in fishing, though his father never failed to utilize every opportunity to encourage him to acquire western education.

At home, food was almost done. Uyaemena had little Obumneke strapped on her back as she prepared lunch. Sitting on a short wooden stool, Uyaemena's legs were stretched and spread in a v shape. With both knees, she held the local mortar firm to the ground. Fair-skinned and oval-faced, there was no beauty in her for any man to desire her. Her wrinkled skin looked like that of an eighty-year-old. Looking at her face, arms and legs, one would wish she had a thicker coating of flesh that would be proportionate to the skeletal layout that made up her frame. Years of economic scourge and social brouhaha added up to eclipse any remaining trace of charm and attraction about her. More years of toiling in the farms and open market under extreme weather conditions combined to be the final nail in the coffin of her lustre and elegance.

Bare-footed, her garment consisted of a faded but clean blouse and a wrapper around her waist. Baby Obumneke was crying and struggling with all her energy, determined to break loose from her mother's apron strings. Uyaemena was overseeing too many things at the same time. While pounding the mass of cooked cassava in the mortar, she had to stand now and again to go and regulate the fireplace. Her pot of soup, almost ninety percent cooked, was on the tripod in the fireplace.

Obumneke's nose had a stream of mucus making a downward movement towards her upper lip. Time and again, the child used her tongue to aid the movement of that creamy mucus into her mouth. She seemed to be reminding anyone who cared that if she was strapped to her mother's back, her tongue was not bound. Obviously, she seemed to enjoy the taste of that mucus. If not for anything, that stream of mucus helped to soothe the little baby. Anytime she put her tongue to work, her cry was punctuated.

"Good afternoon, Ma!" Clinton greeted.

"Welcome home, my son! How was school today?"

"Fine, Ma. The only snag about school is that every pupil who has not paid his school fees shall not be allowed into the classroom tomorrow. That was exactly what I was trying to remind Papa about this morning."

"Be patient until he comes back home. You know your daddy does not joke about your education."

"Yes, Mama; he says I will go to very big schools in the city and train to be a lawyer. He says we have no lawyer in the family who can represent us when we have problems with the oil company."

"Yes, my son! That's the spirit! Don't play with your academics. Very soon, you'll become a very big man in the community. When you become a lawyer, I will become Mama lawyer."

"And I'll buy a big car and build a good house for you and Papa."

"Yes, my son."

"And I'll take Obumneke and Nnabuenyi to the big city."

"You may now go in and change your garments."

Not long afterwards, Egonakpari came home. He ought to be happy that he'd be able to settle some of his outstanding financial obligations, but he was at the same time sad. He had received his salary, but he might as well begin to borrow anew and buy on credit if he paid everything he owed from the previous month. Uyaemena observed that the countenance of her husband was not cheerful. She knew this was his regular mien whenever he received his salary. Before his salary was paid, Egonakpari would hope and pray for it to be paid. However, when it was eventually paid, it always produced a reaction different from what was expected. He always seemed to remember all his woes once he had that envelope in his hand. He always looked happier at those times when he hoped salaries would soon be paid. Today, he wore that same melancholic disposition of his.

"My husband, what's the problem this time?"

"Nothing new, my wife. It is the same old problem of one being a pauper amid plenty."

"Take it easy. Very soon, things will definitely change for the better."

"I know the problem with me. It is squarely a problem of destiny. I believe that God created every other human being. Possibly, in the process of creation, he went into his bedroom to pick an item when suddenly one of his servants, who had been watching him create, hurriedly packaged me and put me in my mother's womb. That servant must have forgotten to assign me my own portion of the blessings of life. That explains why all my efforts to succeed always end up in futility."

"How dare you think that way! Are you worse off in life than all others?"

"Could you please name one man who is worse off than I am?"

"There are equal opportunities for everybody. The truth is that you are very conservative and afraid to take any risk. Risk-takers change their situations for the better. Go inside, eat, rest, and think of what to do with your life, our lives. You better stop speaking that way lest you infest the entire family with such miserable mentality."

Before Uyaemena served dinner that evening, Egonakpari brought out his pay packet and literally divided it in parts: some for different creditors; Clinton's school fees and PTA levy; house upkeep allowance for Uyaemena, and a few other things. He was virtually left with nothing for exigencies. But such a situation was not new in Egonakpari's home. It had become the norm, not the exception. Invariably, he'd find a means to survive until the next payday.

No sooner had Egonakpari sat down to eat than he received a radio alert to the effect that there was an outbreak of fire within Well 016. Shocked at the news, he mistakenly upturned the table on which his dinner was served, wasting the entire plate of pounded fufu with fresh vegetable soup and stormed out of the house. He had gone some 100 meters before he realized that he didn't have any shirt on. He made a U-turn, sped back to the house, picked the first outer garment he saw and re-embarked on his race to the well location.

As he approached the scene of the fire, he was overwhelmed by the enormity of the conflagration. Community folks who gathered there were of little or no assistance. The ferocious manner in which the flame raged, increasing in size and spreading to nearby farmlands and ponds, made it rather difficult for the rural dwellers to risk fighting to bring the fire under control. Rather, they bemoaned the apparent loss of their crops, and feared a possible sacking of the entire community in the event of Niger Oil not being able to control the fire, and timely too. It was obvious that a spillage had started earlier, and was either not detected on time, or was deliberately ignored due to some human error or oversight. As a follow-up, some careless activity had ignited a fire which now spread as it trailed the route of the fore-running liquid.

Soon enough, Egonakpari sent and received as many radio messages as he could. Much damage had been done before the fire-fighting staff and equipment of Niger Oil were finally mobilized to site. It took close to seventy-two hours before the inferno was finally brought under control. Some farms and a few houses were destroyed in the process. Ponds and rivers were also polluted as the spillage forced its way through these. Though no life was lost, many were rendered homeless. A few others had their means of livelihood totally cut off.

For nearly seven days, men whose farms, ponds and homes had been affected besieged the premises of Niger Oil, seeking to know the official position of the oil firm and what it would likely portend for them. It was not until a fortnight after the fire outbreak that a combined team of environmentalists arrived for an assessment. They were made up of biochemists, soil scientists, aquaculture practitioners, socio-economists, and air quality experts drawn from the Federal Environmental Protection Agency, the State Ministry of Environment, Niger Oil, and some independent scholars.

The team was officially welcomed by the Land Area Manager. Breaking his tradition, The Land Area Manager personally came out to welcome the team. They were treated to a sumptuous lunch. Each of the twelve inspectors was given an envelope containing five thousand dollars. The Land Area Manager reminded them that Niger Oil was in business to make a profit and help develop Nigeria. He also stated that the oil firm had been a responsible corporate citizen and had obviously been contributing to moving the nation forward. Niger Oil provided six Toyota Hilux utility vehicles to assist the visiting team in their movement.

In the commencement of their assignment, the team visited the location of well 016, the starting point of the fire. Here, they made observations and took air and soil samples. They were led by the Land Area Manager. Thereafter, they proceeded to several other spots, going as far as the fire had spread, making more observations, and taking samples of water, air, and soil as they advanced. In three hours, they were through with their observations and sample collections.

As part of their itinerary, they visited the village head of Adagalaba community, Chief Illona Oshimili. The leader of the visiting team, Professor Dufuemba Anyaukwu, an environmental consultant with the National Environmental Protection Agency, thanked the community for their co-operation with the government and with Niger Oil. He relayed the Federal Government's goodwill message to the community. It was because of the strategic position of Adagalaba, he said, that the Federal Government assembled such a high-powered team for the job.

Professor Anyaukwu added that it was unfortunate, however, that some enemies of progress were at work to slow down the wheel of progress in that community. Specifically, he said that preliminary studies had shown that the fire outbreak was a result of sabotage.

He promised that, in due time, the team would collate the results and produce a comprehensive report which would be submitted to the Federal Government, with copies made available to the state government, Niger Oil, and Adagalaba Community Development Union.

Chief Illona Oshimili, responded accordingly. He cleared his throat and expressly thanked the team for their work. Then he said, "My friends, I do not understand the callousness of the governments, whether at the federal, state, or local level. I am also not blind to the insensitivity of Niger Oil executives. It is sad to note that such colossal damage was done to our community, and to date, no palliative measure has been adopted by any of the three tiers of government. It took our governments two whole weeks to send a team to assess the damage. To date, no government official has come to visit. I and my people are now fully aware that all the various governments and Niger Oil want from Adagalaba are the oil and gas that they keep drilling from our land.

"We know you do not care about us in any way whatsoever. However, I have two messages for you. One is for both the federal government and Niger Oil, while the other is strictly for the government. The first message is that my community shall not continue to allow themselves to be fooled again and again. From today, be it known to you that my people and I will henceforth decide on who is permitted to drill oil from our land. We will defend our resources with everything we have at our disposal.

"Secondly, take the message to those irresponsible governments that they must remember that natural gas and oil are non-renewable. Tell them that a time is coming, and very soon for that matter, when there'll no longer be any barrel of oil or cubic meter of gas to come from Adagalaba land or any part of the entire Niger Delta region. I may not live to see that, but that day shall definitely come.

"Since our political leaders have colluded with oil firms to turn the blessings of God and nature into a curse, the consequences of that curse shall come wholly on them and their families. Go back to your paymasters and tell them that we have received their message. We shall now see to it that we faithfully keep our own part of the bargain. Thank you!"

Several years afterwards, there has neither been any official report as promised nor a package of compensation for those who lost their crops and livestock. Adagalaba remains an indictment of the image of corporate Nigeria.

CHAPTER 2.
SISTER MABEL

She was aged twenty-eight, but she was already the branch manager of a leading commercial bank. Excellence International Bank was reputed to be the highest-paying bank in Nigeria in terms of staff salary and allowances. The bank was financially sound. Staff dedication was unrivalled in the industry. These, coupled with the bank's uncompromising commitment to integrity and professional ethics, helped to place the bank on a very high pedestal. She was the manager of Alausa branch of the bank. Alausa is in Ikeja, Lagos state, Southwest Nigeria. Her full name is Mabel Fashanu. Amiable and always very cheerful, her ability to enliven her immediate environment was fantastic. One would wonder if Mabel wouldn't do better as a professional cheerleader than a banker. Yet, in banking, she had done extremely well.

This Mabel! Plump and fair-skinned, she was not tall. She was always elegantly dressed. Whether in her formal suits, in line with the bank's dress code; or in casuals at weekends; or yet in traditional Yoruba *iro* and *buba*, Mabel was always simply charming. Round cherubic-faced, her dentition could not have been better. Her big, brown eyes, always bright, tended to increase Mabel's ability to affect her circle. Affecting her circle and her world, was in line with the vision and mission of the Christian ministry where Mabel had enmeshed her spirit. This vision was the chant: *"making the world a sweeter place"*. She was an active member of Divine Diplomats Church. In these circles, she was called Sister Mabel Fash. And truly, if the sun shone, she brightened up faces.

Divine Diplomats Church is geographically taprooted in Nigeria. Then she had her branches spread out to Europe, North America, South Africa, and later to neighbouring West African countries. The church began operations in a modest hotel banquet hall somewhere in the suburbs of Ikeja. It was like the story of the mustard seed, the story of faith! It was the story of a daring spirit; the story of a believing mind; and the story of a yielded body. A little spark makes a fire! A little leaven! Not negatively, though!

The story of Divine Diplomats Church is intertwined with the story of an enterprising and handsome young man with an impeccable dress sense. He was dashing in his well-tailored suits! I hope you know what this means. He wore top-of-the-range designer labels. Italian leather covenanted with his feet. His hair was always jerry curled. He was a gentleman in the mould of Nathaniel, the Jew. He was a charismatic preacher. Enter Pastor Jay-Jay, leading men and women in high sounding shouts of hallelujah, organizing mega crusades and block-bursting programs and recording the miraculous! He inspired faith, he talked tough, and he commanded respect. "Lord, have mercy! Shout hallelujah! I can do all things!"

Mabel was a worker in the Lord's vineyard. You know? Explicably devoted! What the natural man would call a volunteer worker. All the same, she was a worker. She was working for the Lord, working for Divine Diplomats and working for Pastor Jay-Jay. Nay, she was working with Pastor Jay-Jay. Everybody should be a worker, or that everybody was a worker; that was the pastor's persuasion, argument, and conviction. That was Pastor's philosophy. Ideally, everyone! "When the son of man shall come, would he find some faith on the earth?" He hoped so. Therefore, he taught the people to believe. He taught them to work. He taught them to know. He taught them to depend, to love, and to serve. Sister Mabel did all these, and she always shouted hallelujah.

Working for the Lord meant much. It was much more than working without monthly payslips. It also included but was not limited to giving to the Lord. Your money is you. Umh! Okay! Better coinage: your money represents you. You give yourself first, like Sister Mabel Fash did. In the beginning, they came for her.

They came for her soul, her lost soul and her condemned spirit. Her sins were many. They were very heavy. They weighed her down. Those sins! How her spirit bent and walked in a bowed-over fashion. She needed a miracle. She needed a spiritual miracle to straighten her up. She needed a soul-cleansing miracle.

Yet, she was lucky. No, she was blessed. Yes! She was richly blessed that salvation was there with them. They had brought salvation on a silver platter. No! He had walked in there himself. He was seated with them. This salvation! All she needed to do was say 'yes.' Affirmation of faith! Oh! How big and heavy her burden of sin. "Come unto me, all ye that labour and are heavy laden. I will give you rest." The attraction was strong. It was in her interest to yield; to let go. After all, the demons lurked around. Lucifer was there, roaring, ready to devour.

Rejection of this free offer was an invitation to the demonic host: those malevolent rebels for whom a place was not found in heaven but enjoying the privilege and honour of eternal reservation of the hottest region of that lake of fire. Was it not normal for those demons to take the human deviants with them? Think of it! "Birds of a feather should flock together". They'd enjoy living together. But here, right here in the restaurant was the cross. Calvary was transported to *Agidingbi;* to Bonny kitchen. "Great is the mystery of godliness". They'd gone there for lunch. But Calvary was there. It was a pool of blood. Here, the repentant is washed. The sinner is cleansed. He is cleansed and made whole. So, Mabel gave her life.

It was her spirit that was being courted. That was in the beginning. Then her services were needed. Mabel was groomed. Thereafter, she became Sister Mabel Fash. How good she felt when addressed that way. It was one Wale! Yes, Brother Wale! He started this stylish address. From Mabel Fashanu, he christened her Mabel Fash.

It spread so much that everybody now called her Mabel Fash. They taught her the importance of attending meetings. They termed those meetings "fellowship meetings"! They brought forth their strong reasons: "iron sharpens iron"; and again: "not forsaking the assembling of ourselves together". They kept strengthening: do not be unequally yoked. Sister Mabel had yielded her spirit and her body. But her mind? Yes! Her mind must totally submit also. The declaration was in relation to the spirit, and the attendance to the body. But then, "where your money or your treasure is, there will your mind be also".

Sister Mabel Fash got the leading. Oh yes! The Lord gave everything. He owns everything. "He owns the cattle on a thousand hills". How true! Yet how strange! It was strange to think that the Lord of the Christians owned all the cattle in the world. Well, the book was inspired. It is free from error. It is the very thought of God. You must believe it to be saved. Sister Mabel believed. Since he owned all, was it not reasonable and wise, and tending to holy living if one gave back to God all that belonged to Him? Oh! The naturally obvious absurdity of the other side of that coin: "give and it shall be given unto you". "Cast your bread upon the waters, and after many days, it will come back to you".

Mabel did cast her bread upon the waters. Loaf after loaf! Her bread! Her money! The work of the Lord, the ministry, was the waters. She gave because she believed. It wasn't easy, though. The struggle for Sister Mabel's money was almost as strong as the struggle for her soul. The battle was being fought in her mind. The forces of giving were arraigned against the forces of self-gratification. The forces of faith were pitched against the forces of reason. It was the foolishness of God versus the wisdom of man. But Brother Wale and other brothers and sisters were always around Mabel. They were visiting all the time: in person; in dreams and visions; through telephone calls. How they cared!

What about Pastor Jay-Jay? His argument was a hammer, breaking every resistance into pieces. He never visited, though. He was preoccupied with the work: with prayers; with counselling; with preaching;

and with teaching, saving the lost and strengthening the weak; the weak like Sister Mabel Fash. The hammer of the pastor's argument came strongly upon the mind of Sister Mabel Fash. "Your prosperity depended on your giving; where you are today is a result of how you gave yesterday." Vintage Pastor Jay-Jay! He had the gift of the gab. He was a persuasive preacher, anointed of the Lord. And Sister Mabel Fash will join the congregation to sing:

I give it shall be given unto me
I give it shall be given unto me
I give it shall be given unto me
Good measure, pressed down, and running over!

When youth, faith, and emotionality meet, the fervency of spiritual fire is unparalleled. Divine Diplomats boasted the highest concentration of youthfulness in single Christian congregations across the length and breadth of Nigeria. Like a well-run football team, they had feeder teams in almost all tertiary institutions in Nigeria. *Diplomatic Passion* is the satellite fellowship arm charged with the responsibility of catching them young. Upon graduation, each member is furnished with addresses of branches of the church in major cities across the country.

Exceptional organizational skill, ability to influence, and miracle-working faith met themselves in Pastor

Jay-Jay. On Sundays, streams of young men and women always flowed in. Some were upwardly mobile, already calling the shots in their business cocoons; others were struggling and believing, hoping that tomorrow would bring forth better things; some others were in despondent situations - hopeless, yet coming to wait. They were waiting on the Lord. Probably He'd have mercy. They were a mixed multitude: the righteous, the good, and the wicked.

Soon the pews were full. Opening prayers: taking authority over the host of hell. Now the sick and the needy: remembering them. Alleluia! Amen! Praise the Lord! Then music and dancing time came. They were called to the dance floor. There was rhythmic movement of waists; lifting of assumed holy hands, jumping and shouting. Acrobatic displays! Dancing styles! The beats: reggae, calypso, rock. The environment became charged.

There was a change to sweet melodies. The blues: soul touching. The tempo of spiritual activity was reduced. There was lowering of steps and reduction of noise. Quiet sounds of hallelujah! Groans and moans! "Oh! Yes, Lord! Bless you, Lord! Thank you, dear Lord Jesus!" Sporadic polysyllabic sounds! Language of the Spirit: "the natural man cannot understand these. They are foolishness to him". However, those born of the spirit were communicating with the spirit.

Everyone took their seats again. You could see that the spiritually excited crowd wanted more of this tonic, more of this casting-off of burdens and rejoicing in the presence of the Lord. Here, there's fullness of joy. Living in this place is safety assured. You could still hear a few moans. Shouts and groans interrupted the blessed quietness. Now the choir came up. That was organized singing. It brought about an involuntary response from the congregation, some standing up again, some others humming the tune, even when they never heard it before; you know, kind of being spiritually led. "As many as are led by the spirit, they are the sons of God". Sons and daughters of men are all sons of God. Strangely sweet!

The pastor came up and took the centre stage. He raised a new song. Praises rose to the height of the heavens. Now the pastor spoke; "Praise the Lord!" The hallelujah resounded again and again. Sister Mabel and others were seated, waiting for the word. The word gives life. Then Pastor Jay-Jay leaned on the pulpit, his eyes on thousands of faces in the congregation.

"Praise the Lord, somebody!" he urged.

"Ha-lle-lu-iah!" the entire congregation chorused.

•

"I'm persuaded to introduce this: The Lord's been laying this burden on my heart. Several times also, I have tried to resist, but I am now ready to yield."

"We're going on television soon," he added.

Excitement! Shouts of "hallelujah" rent the air.

"Say it, Pastor!" somebody blasted from the congregation.

"Yes, sir!

"That's right!"

"Ride on, Pastor!"

These phrases and more came from different lips, almost simultaneously. The pastor kept his silence, observing those reactionary utterances, gauging the pulse of the church. He deduced that the verbal support might translate to more solid encouragement.

He continued, "... but it will take some sacrifice."

There was some hush now. The excitement level dropped. Pastor Jay-Jay noticed that and accordingly changed gear.

"The Lord is in need of partners," he continued.

"Who is ready to partner with the Lord to the place of abundance?"

He asked.

"God's looking for a man. He's looking for someone to bless. God's looking for a man who'll say, 'here am I, send me'", he further explained.

That was Pastor Jay-Jay. He did change the minds of members of the congregation. He inspired faith in Mabel and a whole lot of others. He inspired faith in them to essentially and impulsively give beyond their ability.

The pastor continued, "Our programmes on television shall be the very best in Africa. We have the spirit of excellence. Excellence must be the hallmark of everything we do. Our message is unique. We must take this message everywhere. We must take our gospel to every nook and cranny of Nigeria. Europe must hear our message. U.S.A., Canada and the rest of Africa must hear this message. God is asking us to do this, and we must do it.

"We'll sponsor this gospel to Europe and other parts of the world. We have the money. Whatever money God gives you, he gives primarily for the advancement of the gospel. In that case, never make the mistake of thinking that you are the owner of all the money in your account. Don't fall into that trap. You are only a custodian of God's money. Get him involved in your financial planning. Let his Holy Spirit lead you in that area also."

"Now listen," the pastor's facial expression got tenser and firmer. "Listen very carefully," he advised. "The biggest investment you could make is kingdom investment. The best place to put your money and expect unlimited dividends is the gospel. Don't hold back. Your gift to God makes a way for you. Some of you are in terribly poor financial states today because of your refusal to give in the past. And some of those you considered foolish because of how generously they gave keep on being richly blessed every day. See proof of this in Proverbs, chapter eleven, verse twenty-four."

He read. "There is that scattereth, and yet increaseth; and there is that withholdeth more than is meet, but it tendeth to poverty."

Pastor Jay-Jay continued; "I, therefore, urge you to give. Be a financial partner with God and open doors of financial blessings unto yourself. God is faithful. Look at the thirty-eighth verse of the sixth chapter of the book of Luke." He read again from the Bible, and afterwards continued.

"Does it not naturally sound foolish? How is it that it is only when you give that it is also given unto you? But more importantly, he gives you to the point of overflow.

"This morning, we have to take the very first steps of faith. We must raise the equivalent of two million dollars for television and internet broadcast of our programmes. We are already discussing with several stations of the National Television Authority. We are also discussing with several private television stations. The response we are getting is wonderful. We are able. I know we are well able."

He raised a song:
I can do all things

Through Christ which strengthens me
I can do all things
Through Christ
I can do all things
By his resurrection power
I can do all things
Through Christ.

The congregation joined in the song. As they sang, the pastor's voice could be heard through the loudspeakers. He encouraged the congregation:

"We can truly do all things.

Yea! Nothing is impossible!

There's no limit to what we can do.

We get limited only when we think we cannot.

'Believe in the Lord your God,

And you shall be established.

Believe His prophets, and you shall prosper'.

See it!"

He turned the pages of his bible and said, "That wonderful scripture is lifted from the twentieth verse of 2 Chronicles, chapter twenty. How many of you here are willing to give two million naira each? If the good Lord is leading you to sow a seed of two million naira into this project, kindly obey his voice and step forward. Two million naira! Don't rationalize, now! Don't think of things you have planned to do with the money. Prove God now! He'll open the windows of heaven and pour his blessings on you. Create a door for a continuous flow of God's blessings into your life."

It only took the childlike and unfettered, wholehearted acceptance of one man to open the floodgate to other souls. No sooner had Pastor Jay-Jay perfectly linked financial and material prosperity to giving, and asked for specific amounts in pledges, than a young man, relatively unknown in the congregation, opened his briefcase, took out his cheque-book, and wrote the seven-digit figure: two million naira (N2,000,000).

He stood up and walked towards the platform. As the young man approached the pulpit, the congregation roared. The atmosphere became charged with excitement. Then men began to emerge from different sections of the auditorium, following his example. Consequently, a pattern of continuous clapping of hands spontaneously erupted. The hand-clapping was at once a way of hailing the daring spirits of those men, and of giving praise to God for raising men who'd overlook all odds to give to him.

When it became obvious that besides the one and a half dozen men who identified with the two-million-naira figure, nobody was ready and willing to come out again, Pastor Jay-Jay lowered the stakes to a million naira. A larger number of men trooped out. Then he further descended to five hundred thousand naira. Many more people responded. He continued this way until he came to a thousand naira. That was the least amount mentioned as acceptable. At that level, even the unemployed and deprived had faith to respond.

Meanwhile, Mabel was seated, making a. mental calculation of the various financial commitments she was obliged to meet. Only recently, she had assured Jide, her younger sibling, that she'd sponsor his planned immigration to the United States of America. Sponsoring Jide's proposed trip was not just about paying for his flight ticket. It involved that and more. Jide had been frantically exploring possible means of setting his foot in the United States. As far as he was concerned, he didn't care a hoot about the legality or otherwise of his intended action. He had been approached to pay some seven thousand U.S. dollars as fees to enable him to register for a Christian conference tagged as Global Christian Congress. Global Christian Congress is a biennial conference where Christians from different geo-political backgrounds converge to appraise the state of Christianity globally, while at the same time offering postulations on the way forward.

Jide knew little or nothing about the bible and Christianity. He intended to go, not because he desired to participate in the conference, but because he saw it as an avenue to achieving his desire of immigrating to the United States. The recipient of the money,

Reverend Sola Onuma, is the African representative of Global Christian Congress. Reverend Onuma had an elaborate arrangement for picking out those in Jide's category from Guatemala to Belize. If they eventually got to Belize, they'd then spend between six and nine months in that country. Thereafter, he'd devise means of trafficking them into the United States, preferably through Mexico.

Besides sponsoring Jide's proposed trip, Mabel was also paying for the new Range Rover Evoque she acquired on forty-eight-month payment terms. She was well paid, but even before her salary was due, she had often made a very detailed plan of what to do with the money. But Pastor Jay-Jay's words were always strong. Today, he particularly said about those being led by God not to rationalize, and not to think of those things they had earlier planned to do with their money. The banker's instinct in Sister Mabel strongly objected to such. In her mental reasoning, she considered it a subtle method of extortion in the name of God. But the little faith in her, like the mustard seed, was raring to go. She was torn, as always.

Was she being selfish with her money and ungrateful to God? Could this really be a true test? Perhaps something horrible, something sinister might also happen to her as a result of her refusal to give. What about her life? Was it not described as a vapour that vanishes in no time? Giving to God might keep her from sickness, from danger, from death, and from diabolic plans of the wicked. On the other hand, what would become of the dozen issues which had been crying out for financial attention from her? Amidst all these, men and women were trooping out to identify with the call. Finally, she quietly opened her handbag and took out her chequebook. Then she scribbled on a page, "one million naira only".

Such typified fund-raising in *Divine Diplomats*. Sister Mabel was now quite enmeshed in the entire web. She'd regularly pay her tithe. The tithe was God's own money in the Christian's possession. Ten percent of everything the Christian earned, Pastor Jay-Jay taught, belonged to God. Besides the tithe, there were regular offerings. In every meeting, Mabel and other brethren in the house of faith were taught "not to appear before God empty-handed". Further down, the congregation was broken into several micro units called Shepherd Care Microns (S.C.M.). These microns primarily served the purpose of ensuring integration among members of a unit. This way, everybody was made to have a sense of belonging. They got proud of *Divine Diplomats*. A real family-like bond existed among unit members. Pastor Jay-Jay had taught the congregation that one's Christian brother or sister was more closely related to him or her than a blood brother.

Truly, these young men and women in *Divine Diplomats* had a lot of things going for them. Pastor Jay-Jay himself was a symbol of charismatic Christianity. He was a role model to millions of disillusioned young men and women in a country where the majority of the citizenry had been battered by the demons of socio-economic penury. The kernel of his message truly pointed these disillusioned, hopeless, and devalued human beings to some better life - something close to earthly utopia. Athletic, his mind was steely, determined to achieve set goals and objectives; and his spirit was daring, seeing possibilities his peers would rather shake off as unattainable. He made some otherwise timid and cringing human beings suddenly rediscover the essence of their existence. He inspired faith in them. This faith produced inner strength and outward boldness.

On the physical front, he was a power dresser. The law of reproduction was at work here. It was no wonder, then, seeing a similar pattern evolve among members of his congregation. Not that those members competed against one another. However, a Sunday in *Divine Diplomats* was like seeing a thousand and one models promoting the same number of designer labels. Whilst a good percentage actively participated in these fashion statements, the economically struggling ones among them looked more like visitors who had come to see the fair and possibly see how the same could be of benefit to them.

Mabel Fash was at home with *Divine Diplomats*. She ranked among the best dressed in the congregation. Part of her ambition was to be among the very toppers in financial partnership. Being a financial partner meant setting aside some percentage of one's income for sponsorship of *Diplomatic Television*. Pastor Jay-Jay had taught that being a soul-winner was not just all about going to the field physically. When one invested his money, and souls were won to Christ through the instrumentality of his money, such a person was equally a soul-winner. To Sister Mabel and others, that was a rather simplified method of getting a star-studded crown reserved for a saint when he or she finally transited to heaven. Most people want very easy access to heaven.

Among other things, Sister Mabel also learnt that "money answereth all things". True! She believed that money could do just about anything. Money! A type of god to be worshipped, eulogized and courted for its numerous favours; or a talisman to crack hard nuts, mesmerize and intimidate real and imagined enemies. Mabel was now irrevocably committed to the work of *Divine Diplomats*. She soon became a financial partner, committing thirty percent of her monthly remuneration to this cause. That was besides her tithes, offerings, and other contributions which benefitted the *Divine Diplomats Church*.

The more she gave, the more compelled she felt to give. Letters began to pour in from different departments and branches of the Ministry, thanking her for rendering one assistance or the other; for answering the Macedonian call (to help); inviting her to a fund-raising dinner or luncheon. She soon became a household name, not only in *Divine Diplomats Churches* all over the city of Lagos but also in *Diplomatic Passion* chapters in tertiary institutions. Whenever she identified any need, she'd immediately respond. Church was priority number one.

Soon, she lost her sense of financial planning. Mabel began to take advantage of her position to take loans from the bank. She was smart enough to manipulate some customers into using their names to ask for such facilities on her behalf. She was the Branch Manager, she always assured them. They'd not be harassed by the bank. And they weren't harassed early enough. For the length of time that she remained the Manager, no such harassment was envisaged. She contributed so much to the cause of Divine Diplomats Church that Pastor Jay-Jay had to write a special letter of appreciation to her. Moreover, she quickly climbed the ladder to become the Vice President of the Inner Court, an elitist Shepherd Care Micron.

On the family front, Mabel began to withdraw from family issues she had earlier considered her responsibility. Every passing day, she became more estranged from her biological family and secular friends. She also reneged on her earlier promise to bankroll Jide's trip to the United States. Moreover, she also developed the unenviable habit of always abandoning her duty post, abusing the process of delegacy. Mabel, hitherto known for her conscientiousness and meticulousness in the bank, was now becoming the very opposite of her former endearing personal profile. Her colleagues in the bank wondered what was wrong with Mabel. Those who managed to ask were sharply rebuffed. Her life, she always told them, was nobody else's business.

Mabel became entangled in some intricate web of difficulties. She had run into some serious indebtedness. Internal auditors had queried Alausa branch. Mabel's unsatisfactory answers prompted an invitation to the Disciplinary Committee at Head Office. Consequently, she was asked to proceed on forced leave while an official from Head Office was drafted in as the acting Branch Manager. The assumption of duty by the new official opened a can of worms. Within a few weeks, details of Mabel's unorthodox practices in the bank were unearthed.

One thing followed another in quick succession. The bank invited Mabel to yet another meeting. At the meeting, she was duly handed over to detectives from the Economic and Financial Crimes Commission (EFCC).

"Miss Fashanu!" Mr Michael Tejuosho addressed her in a rather cracked and subdued voice. He was the Assistant General Manager, Branch Operations.

"Your rise in this bank has been rather meteoric. We all have been very proud of you. For two consecutive years, you won the bank manager of the year award, an honour every banker would dream of. You never compromised your position. You were totally committed and focused until recently. The entire management is dumbfounded. I sincerely do not understand the sudden metamorphosis you have undergone. Well, it is very unfortunate that the bank cannot stop regulatory agencies and the police from carrying out their statutory and constitutional function. We'll closely monitor the developments. Good morning!"

Mabel was moved to be the guest of Special Criminal Investigations Department, Alagbon Close, Ikoyi, while investigations into the alleged fraud continued. The initial reaction of members of Divine Diplomats was that of empathy. Some displayed some rare sense of sharing her sorrow. Some members of the Inner Court Shepherd Care Micron and a few other members of the larger church visited Mabel. Detained alongside Mabel were two young men through whom she had secured loans for what she called "kingdom investment".

For a few weeks, Mabel was the subject of much of the gossip, not only within Excellence International Bank but also among members of Divine Diplomats. The Press swooped on the story and accorded it prominence in their reporting that fateful week. The church swiftly reacted. *Divine Diplomats Church* called a press conference in which her spokesman utterly condemned the "morally disgusting and fundamentally embarrassing practice of Miss Mabel Fashanu." While acknowledging that Mabel regularly worshipped with them, and that Mabel, like every other member, made generous contributions in cash and kind to advance the course of the gospel, the church took strong exceptions to being linked, directly or remotely, with the sins of Mabel Fashanu.

The church, the spokesman continued, was truly committed to the teaching of holiness, faith, and the love of God. "However," he added, "donations made to God through the Church are non-refundable".

Mabel's fate seemed almost certain. She and her accomplices in crime would most certainly end up in jail.

Mabel herself knew that so much had been damaged by her now uncovered sharp practices. She had already lost her freedom. She was losing her job, losing her fellowship *koinonia* with the brethren and losing her integrity and social acceptance. She lost her face. Being informed of the official position of *Divine Diplomats*, members of the church concomitantly aligned themselves with that position. None visited Mabel at Alagbon again.

Meanwhile, a redemption plan was being hatched by a group of Excellence International Bank's executives for Mabel Fashanu. These men and women had met and decided to contribute money aimed at repaying those loans with conditions attached: that the bank should negotiate and effect the release of Mabel and her accomplices as soon as the money was repaid. They hinged their support and argument on the fact that Mabel didn't really enrich herself but was misled to wrongfully give to the church what was not in her authority to give. The core management accepted the condition but foreclosed the possibility of Mabel's return to the bank.

Twenty-four hours after she had walked out of that detention cell, Mabel received a letter officially informing her that she had been summarily dismissed. Being alone in the house, she lacked the strength to kneel before God. Prior to this time, she seemed to possess this strength in excess. She sauntered out of the house and wended her way through Abiola Crescent in Ikeja. She had no immediate plan for self-rehabilitation. She was confused and lost. Much more psychologically crushing was the fact that she was alone.

In her loneliness, she looked up to the sky, imagining the sitting position of God. Now stationary by the wayside and leaning on a tree, trickles of hot tears rolled down her cheeks. As the rainy season wind roughly caressed her face, she opened her mouth and said, "Father, forgive me. I have disappointed you." She said this, totally oblivious of the presence of Brother Wale, who had defied the official position of the church and had come to commiserate with Mabel Fash.

CHAPTER 3.
LANDSLIDE VICTORY

Chief (Dr) Sinclair Ochonkeya Ebirieze is true to type. A politician of Nigerian hue, he is an Igbo of South-Eastern Nigeria. Ebirieze is not just smart, he is a cat. Sharp-witted and sleek, he makes no pretences about his interest and involvement in politics. He lived the greater part of his life in Houston, Texas, United States of America. He is one black African lucky enough to get enmeshed in the internal oil politics of Texan oil giants in particular, and the United States in general. As a Nigerian, he was one of the facilitators of the deal that put the United States in demand of Nigeria's Bonny Light crude. People who consider themselves informed aver that Ebirieze continues to receive a certain percentage on every barrel of crude oil sold to the Americans.

Besides this, the high chief is involved in illegal oil bunkering. He facilitates the sale of illegally bunkered oil. Not too long ago, he came back home. The community that made up his immediate constituency received news of his homecoming with mixed feelings. It seemed to be good news that this chief had come home, they reasoned. But what actually moved him to come home? He is enigmatic. Nobody could trust him. "The toad," some argued, "does not run in the daytime for nothing: if he is not chasing after something, then something is obviously chasing after him". For a fortnight, Ebirieze's sudden homecoming was the oil that kept the flame of gossip aglow in Atugo town. Not even his blood relations could write a short biography of Ebirieze. He came home alone: no wife, no son, and no daughter. Yet he always talked about his immediate family.

As soon as he returned, he gave himself the "primary assignment" of building a palatial country home. He accomplished this in a record time of eight months. Today, that country home stands out as a magnificent architectural masterpiece. Ebirieze said that, as a politician, he needed to put up such an edifice to earn him some respect. He believed this edifice would play host to several political meetings in the future. His retinue of domestic staff number over a hundred. They include gardeners, cooks, electricians, masons, carpenters, plumbers, launderers, security men, drivers, and others.

Next, he set up a foundation to help the needy. His foundation offered scholarships to a select number of indigent students of tertiary and secondary institutions from Omiemi, his home state. He also contracted some hospitals in his Local Government

Area and earmarked them for his free medical services. His community is predominantly made up of farmers, so Ebirieze boosted farming culture with the' purchase and distribution of light farming implements among hundreds of farmers living in the community. Several farmers were also given soft loans to improve their farms. He also purchased four tractors to aid this farming revolution. Any farmer who intended using one of the tractors only needed to fuel one and use it for no more than twenty-four hours. By so doing, he succeeded in reducing, to some considerable degree, any ill-will harboured against him. Though these deeds put him in a good light, there existed a handful of community folks who felt they could read the biblical handwriting on the wall. They adopted the popular proverb that "he who eats the roasted testicles of a ram is a debtor to hernia". This proverb became the watchword of these folks whenever they were engaged in dissuading others from enjoying Ebirieze's welfare package. To this group, partaking of Ebirieze's philanthropic gestures was more akin to mortgaging their conscience in advance- a Greek gift, so to say. They always tried to interpret every new move the returnee chief made afterwards. They had always heard of his fabulous wealth. Evil reports had always been associated with him also. Rumours of money laundering, involvement in child trafficking and advance fee fraud also made the rounds involving him. Yet he'd never been arraigned in the United States or any other part of the world for any crime.

However, Chief (Dr) Ebirieze was calculating enough. He was aware that the majority of Nigerians were poor. He perfectly understood that his community folks were no better than other Nigerians. He appreciated the value those suffering folks placed on a naira note. Also, he had plenty of dollars; the money he earned during his long sojourn in the United States was more than enough for his needs and those of his so-called immediate family. Yet, he wanted more money. More money! To Ebirieze, money is power. The power to do more! The power to influence! The power to make things happen! Relevance in this part of the world wholly depended on money. However, Ebirieze decided that he was not going to let anybody know that he wanted more money. No, he would simply turn philanthropic. That would help build a good name for him and erase any negativity about his image. That was the reason behind his magnanimity.

He came home at the right time. Since the General Olisiego Okoronjo-led junta handed over political power to civilians almost three years earlier, ending seventeen years of military dictatorship in Nigeria, civilians were now fully in control. This period witnessed adjustments and realignment of political positions and leanings. Soon, the nation would have to transition from one civilian government to another.

Money talks! And in an economy like this, the voice of money is even louder. Ebirieze knew this, so he was determined to put his vast financial resources to work. To Ebirieze, the king is not just the man who sits on an imaginary throne. He is not the existing figurehead devoid of executive powers. The king is the man who can influence the thought pattern and direction of most of his immediate audience or reach. The king is the man who calls the shots. He may not be a leader. He cajoles and threatens. He woos with soft words and barks ferociously when he wishes to. In different societies, certain denominators determine the emergence of kings. In the Nigerian political landscape, money is the major factor. This lesson was not lost to Chief Ebirieze.

To solidify his position in the party, Chief Ebirieze ensured he had access to the political bigwigs at the helm. He made huge financial donations to the campaign of Alhaji Nuhu Waziri, the incumbent president of the Federal Republic of Nigeria, and flagbearer of Masses Democratic Movement. Alhaji Nuhu Waziri is the scion of the most powerful caliphate in the country. Rightly or wrongly, Waziri's family members believe Nigeria is a gift to them, and that they are born to perpetually rule Nigeria. Their grip on power has been long, strong and tight. Part of their strategy for a continuous tenacious hold on power was ensuring that only sworn members of the Hausa-Fulani oligarchy and a few southerners who could easily be bought over with money or positions were appointed as top electoral commission officers. Ebirieze swore allegiance to the Caliphate in exchange for their blessing on his immediate political plan.

Over time, he established contacts and began to attend political meetings in and out of Omiemi state. His financial contributions to these political groups could not be overlooked. He earned a voice among the leading men and women in these groups. Ebirieze was at home with gangsterism. Consequently, he was rather elated to see that, except for a few distinguished men of impeccable character and integrity, the emerging political class of the time was mostly peopled with men of dubious antecedents. They were men who, at best, could be called dishonourable, and at worst, criminals. Though the word "criminal" seems to have assumed a new meaning in his country, crime remains crime if the English lexicon exists.

Those who make bold to get involved in mega-frauds, misappropriation, outright siphoning of public funds and drug business are rather honoured with chieftaincy titles by different communities across the country. This trend continues and is also evidently portrayed by the country's universities. The universities seem to compete with one another on the conferment of honorary doctorate degrees to this same crop of politicians. The voice of money is loud in Nigeria. It is loud, also, in the so-called citadels of learning and centres of academic excellence. University authorities have always alleged that universities are grossly under-funded. Based on this premise, universities devise several means of raising money.

One of such is the commercialization of honorary doctorate degrees. *Vice-chancellors* and governing councils silently agreed to throw decorum to the winds, conferring such honours on men of questionable character and proven intellectual bankruptcy. Such was the prevailing situation when Ebirieze launched his political career.

Political parties have been registered and were directed to open offices in at least two-thirds of the states in the Federal Republic of Nigeria. They were also instructed to spread these offices as geographically wide as possible. Ebirieze was convinced that a farmer who sows during the planting season shall inevitably reap at harvest time. He chose to sow his money in political activity. He became a major financier of the Masses Democratic Movement. In his opinion, when the chips are down, his huge contributions would invariably give him some leverage over others. Besides being involved in the party, Ebirieze also hatched his own personal political plan - a plan aimed at him becoming the next Executive Governor of his state.

Part of this larger plan was the idea of floating a private security outfit. The outfit would be charged with the responsibility of ensuring the chief's personal safety, and derailing, in the manner considered most appropriate and expedient, the programme of any other politician(s) whose political success could automatically spell failure for Ebirieze. He was also doing his utmost to launch his governorship campaign even before others would get to thinking along that line.

"Kololo!" the chief called the head of his security detail as they were being chauffeur-driven in the chief's Cadillac to Okemba, the state capital.

"I'm loyal, sir!" Kololo answered.

"How is the preparation for the launch?"

"Everything is running very smoothly, sir."

"How do you mean?"

"The Divisional Police Officer has given us his word that a hundred and twenty armed policemen shall be drafted to the venue, sir. They are coming from Mobile Police Units in Omiemi and neighbouring states."

"And...?"

"We have also employed the services of the local vigilantes to complement the efforts of the police."

"What about publicity?"

"Radio and television announcements will commence tomorrow. We have already created a website and are reaching millions on the internet. There are billboards, banners and posters strategically placed all over the state."

"What about the boys, Kololo? Time is running out. How is their training progressing?"

"Splendidly, sir!"

"Concretely and concisely, please!"

"They are through with personal defence, decoding of signals, carriage and comportment in public, handling distressing situations, camouflage in enemy territory, elimination method, coded communication, and evacuation methodology. They are currently undergoing intensive training on the use of short- and medium-range weapons."

"How long do you expect it will take them to be through?"

"Five more days, sir. Just as it was originally scheduled."

"I hope your judgment is good."

Job advertisements had earlier been placed in some national newspapers for suitably qualified young men who'd work in a private security outfit, with the promise of very competitive remuneration. Hundreds of young men swallowed hook, line and sinker what they saw in the newspapers. Applications tumbled in daily so that, within a week of the publication, nearly a thousand applications had been received. For two days, Kololo, Madness, and Angela, the chief's personal secretary sorted the applications and short-listed candidates to be invited for interview. They were directed to report to the state secretariat of the Masses Democratic Movement at exactly 9.00 am on a particular Monday.

However, as early as 8.00 am the state secretariat of the political party had become filled with people. The boys, coming in from different parts of the state and from two neighbouring states, had trickled in one after another until a crowd was assembled. Spontaneously, they started a discussion. Bored by inactivity, one of the boys, whose name was Scorpion, started an interactive session.

"But this place na complete fuck-up oh!" he said. "How they come carry us keep here like condemned prisoners?"

"No be the thing wey we dey talk for this our country since be this? Man picken don become mugu for big men dem hand", Charlie quipped.

"Na Naija leaders you go blame. They no fit engineer this country well", Nnanna concurred, identifying those he considered the real culprits.

"But this country get money oh! See as all these politicians and military men dey spend money here and there." That was Bruno.

"This Chief Ebirieze, the way him dey spend money ehn, e be like say him dey print money sef."

"Ah!" added Spider. "This man no make him money for Naija oh! E don tee when we don dey hear say him be big man for America."

"Yes oh!" Jimmy concurred. "The kind brain wey him get ehn, na super brain oh! In short, the man too sharp!"

"The man dey try for Omiemi people too", Jonathan praised. "They say him don make everything free for the people wey dey Atugo, him hometown."

"Hey! na waa for Naija people sef. No be true oh! Me sef I come from the same place with Chief Ebirieze," Orjiakor informed.

"Him dey try oh! But not as people think," Orjiakor corrected.

"Ehn he? If other big men dey like that, our country no for better since?" Jonathan queried again.

"But the thing fit be to use them catch people. We hear say him wan be governor for this our state," Orjiakor opined.

"Think about am! How many politicians dey do this kind thing?" Jonathan insisted.

These young men kept themselves busy discussing the chief and sundry issues. It was well after 10 o'clock when Kololo appeared, wearing a very stern face. He was brisk and business-like, giving an overall impression of a very busy man, and one who believes in punctuality. Trailing Kololo were twenty black Suzuki Vitara automobiles. As they drove in, their horns blared simultaneously in a very deafening manner. All their headlights were on full beam. They speedily circled the open space several times, raising and distributing millions of otherwise tranquil particles of dust. The drivers soon jumped out in military style, leaving the vehicles' doors open, while the engines revved. Kololo walked towards the interviewees and addressed them.

"Good morning, all!"

"Good morning, sir!" they all chorused, awakening to the fact that the business of the day was about to be kick-started.

"Could you please seat yourselves in these vehicles?" he asked, pointing to the Suzuki automobiles.

"Five persons to one car, please. However, let the drivers see your invitation letters before you board. Thank you!"

Having briefed the boys, Kololo wasted no further time at the party secretariat. He boarded a waiting black Mercedes limousine. This was the same car in which he had arrived. Chief Ebirieze was seated on the third row. Kololo joined the driver in front. Within ten minutes, they arrived at the venue of the interview. An advance team of Chief Ebirieze's men had already pre-arranged the venue. The chief alighted and immediately went into the hall. Kololo followed closely behind, while the driver trailed, bringing the chief's suitcase and newspapers with him. Strangely enough, the chief did not exchange pleasantries with anybody. He just walked directly into the hall and sat on a cushion at the rear.

Soon enough, the twenty automobiles arrived with the group of boys. Chief Ebirieze busied himself with last-minute preparations for the exercise. He intended to hire exactly thirty boys for the execution of his immediate political mission. The interview turned out to be a series of tests ranging from stamina checks to psycho-analytical examination of the dynamics of the individuals' mental attitude, personal resoluteness, and courage.

Every applicant was asked to run a race of 1,600 meters. Those who could not finish the race within a specified timeframe had some points deducted from their scoresheet. Thereafter, drinks were brought in.

They included spirits such as whisky, rum, brandy and gin, beer, and non-alcoholic wine. Assorted packets of cigarettes and several wraps of marijuana were also made available. The young men were asked to go and refresh themselves as they chose. However, before they could pick those items, the organizers had devised means of identifying what each person chose to drink and/or smoke. Non-smokers among them, and those who chose not to smoke on that fateful day, were blacklisted. They would not make the list.

The boys were asked to queue up. Madness, a middle-aged aide of the chief, was stationed at the entrance to the hall. Sitting at a desk, his duty was to write down the names of the applicants as they made their way into the hall to pick items of refreshment. The hall was virtually empty but for Chief Ebirieze, who was seated at the far end, pretending to be busy with some other things, when he was carefully monitoring the disposition of the boys. He was observant enough to note the expression on the face of each as they came in. Obviously, most of them did not immediately recognize that the man seated at the far end of the hall was Chief Ebirieze himself. He was dressed in a white T-shirt and a pair of white sports shorts. With a baseball cap on his head, he cut a picture that was quite far removed from his traditional well-cut safari suits. Dressed the way he was today he could have been anybody.

Kololo was stationed at the second door which was being used as an exit for the purpose of the screening exercise. He already had a paper with serialized numbers and columns for the different types of drinks and cigarettes. As each man came out, he'd offer his hand for a handshake and afterwards record what item of refreshment the person had chosen. He did not bother with the names as Madness had earlier matched the names of the interviewees against those serial numbers. Once out, they were directed to another part of the premises to wait. Currently, the boys were hungry and thirsty.

Later, they were assembled for an oral session. The organizers kept it simple. Everybody was asked the same set of questions. However, there was an excellent level of control over the boys. As soon as any was interviewed, Madness handed an envelope to him, directing him to the waiting room while the interview of others continued. That way, no one yet to be interviewed was able to consult those interviewed before him.

The questions were basically tailored to extract information on their marital status, educational/academic involvement, and parental background (which helped to throw some light on their likely social status). The chief had confessed his preference for boys from broken homes, single parents, non-committed Christian families, and very indigent homes. The chief said boys whose emotional disposition at the time of interview betrayed desperation to succeed and enthusiasm to work were usually very daring and willing to experiment with odd jobs. They also formed the majority of criminals and social hoodlums in the country. Yet, he was quick to add that he didn't wish to demonise a community or social group, but that he was guided by current statistics. He flatly stamped his disapproval of young men who exhibited their willingness to further their education. At the end of the exercise, it was obvious that the right candidates for the project were readily available.

Not too much later, Madness sauntered towards the applicants and asked them to go and board the waiting cars. They were driven to a popular fast-food restaurant where they had lunch. They were asked to report at the MDM secretariat the following Saturday to confirm the interview results. On a designated Wednesday, all successful candidates reported at the same old venue. The chief was on the premises yet concealed enough to escape the glare of his newest employees. The onus fell on Kololo and Madness to brief the young men on their new portfolios. Madness was the first to speak. He formally informed the newly recruited young men that their job was political. Yet, he was careful enough not to give the details as that was under Kololo's jurisdiction. Madness informed the employees that it was for them, and solely for them that the chief was considering getting involved in politics. He addressed them, employing traditional Masses Democratic Movement salutation:

Madness: M.D.M.!

Others: Power!

Madness: M.D.M.!

Others: Power to the people!

Madness: My brothers! It is a new morning! *I say it is a new morning! I say day don break for us. As our country dey today, una like am?*

Others: No o o!

Madness: *"Me sef, I no like am. We have been praying and fasting; crying and weeping. Today! I say today, God don answer our prayer. Our big brother wey be Chief (Dr) Sinclair Ebirieze don agree sey him go come help make this country better. Make una reason am well well. Him don talk say na him money him go spend. We know say him get money nyafu! No be for obodo America wey him dey since for to do business? Him gidigba for ground. Him don talk say him go match dem dollar for naira; power for power; oyibo for oyibo. Chief tell us say na bicos of poor people him come.*

"Him been talk say him no like as poor people dey suffer for this our obodo Nigeria. And our people wey be Igbo, him don talk say other tribes dey marginalize us. A bi dat word too big? E mean dem dey cheat us, take the thing wey belong to us share for themselves. Whether dem like it or not, na chief go become the next executif govano for this Omiemi State. Him say him wan waka first before him go run. After govanoship, ehn hen, him go catch other big, big positions, including for to be president for this our obodo Naija. But him never announce am oh! That is why una dey here today. Na una go be his first men. Una go work with am. Una go de follow am go campaign. Him go pay una well o! When him become govano, una wey dey here go become special people wey know govano well. I wan invite my brother Kololo make him come finish the talk. Make una listen to am well well. God bless una."

Hip! Hip!! Hip!!!

Others: Hurray!

Madness: M.D.M.!

Others: Power!

Madness: Brother Kololo! Over to you oh!

When Madness was done, Kololo came to the front and addressed the young men.

"Brothers! Good morning! I want to thank Uncle Mad for his brief speech. We have a mission - the mission to support the aspiration of our elder brother,

Chief Sinclair Ebirieze. He has to rule this state. When things get better here, life will be happier for everybody. You will be properly trained on how to handle weapons. We are not training you to kill. We are only equipping you with arms for proper defence of yourself and the team in the unlikely event of any ugly incident. You must show yourself courageous and bold. We will arm and protect you.

"The police shall work with you. We are already in discussions with them. But whatever we do must be enclosed within our minds. No outsider hears it. That is why we ensured that none of you is married. Keep your girlfriends out of this. Food, drinks and cigarettes will be provided daily, free of charge. Besides that, you'll be paid fortnightly. We have no working hours. The chief is providing accommodation for every one of us in his country home. Whenever we follow him out and spend the night, we will be appropriately accommodated and paid our travelling allowances. You may be required to travel at short notice. We have already secured membership cards of Masses Democratic Movement for every one of you.

Since you submitted three passport photographs each, one each was used to procure your cards. Though we are card-carrying party members, our primary job is with EBIRIEZE VANGUARD. That's our name. After this address, go, sign and pick up your uniforms and boots for a brief training session. Thank you!"

On the day of the formal launch of Chief Ebirieze's political project, several cars were lined up. There were so many other cars belonging to party men and friends of Chief Ebirieze who had come to witness this historic launch. The airwaves were filled with announcements of this event. Posters and banners colourfully adorned Okemba, the state capital, and Atugo, the chief's hometown and venue of the launch. MDM top-shots from within and outside the state also came in appreciable numbers to honour the chief. The motorcade extended from the chief's house to Community Secondary School, Atugo, a distance stretching more than a kilometre.

At the launch venue, a live band was stationed, playing some popular highlife tunes. Several traditional dance groups could be seen entertaining the crowd. Different melodies filled the air.

When the chief's entourage drove in, the black Mercedes limousine and those twenty Suzuki cars pulled up as the uniformed political thugs jumped out, taking positions very close to the central canopy which was providing cover for very important personalities.

The limousine, however, drove right to the front of that canopy and pulled up. At this point, the mammoth crowd became wild and hysterical.

The chief alighted. He was clad in a spotless white safari suit with a pair of black shoes to match. He raised the white horse- tail in his right hand. Tumultuous shouts of *"Odozi-obodo 1"* rent the air. Speaker after speaker eulogized the chief. Finally, Ebirieze himself was called upon to speak. When he had duly observed protocols, he made a very brief but articulate speech. The summary was that he was in politics because the cry of his people had reached his ears. He compared his mission to that of Moses of biblical fame - that as Moses was called by Jehovah to deliver the children of Israel from the cruel hands of Pharaoh, he, Ebirieze, has a divine mandate to deliver the Federal Republic of Nigeria. As Moses had to start with individuals who questioned his authority and his mission, he, Ebirieze, would also start his rescue mission from Omiemi state. He said he was fully aware that some of the people he had come to deliver would neither understand nor accept him.

However, he added that whatever the case might be, he, as a true Christian, was ready to carry his cross and go about this God-given assignment until victory was assured. To end his speech, he raised a song:

Until I reach my goal
Until I reach my goal
I will never, ever stop my journey half-way
Until I reach my goal

Ebirieze truly left no stone unturned in his quest for political power. He wanted to wrest the governorship from the incumbent. The incumbent, by reason of his performance over the past three years, had obviously endeared himself to the people of Omiemi State. Therefore, Ebirieze knew he had to task his mind speedily. He also had to masterfully execute every well-articulated plan. He saw the main election as the hurdle before him. All the prospective candidates hitherto warming up in his party, the M.D.M., had been settled. "Settlement" is the Nigerian euphemism for offering monetary inducement and/or firm promises of juicy political appointments to an opponent. This would compel the opponent to withdraw from the race and align his forces with those of the man who settled him. The chief had already shared the cabinet portfolios among such settled opponents, strong party members, and supporters. As far as he was concerned, the upcoming primaries were mere formalities for the endorsement of chosen candidature.

There was only one person Ebirieze trusted as far as political game was involved. That person was himself. He would openly commend friends and supporters for their loyalty, but within the chambers of his heart, he really did not trust anybody. He knew he was self-centred, but the picture he often wanted to paint of himself was that of a caring, altruistic philanthropist. To a large extent, also, he had succeeded in deceiving some of the people. Even among those who worked closely with him, executing his crooked plots, his speech and actions oftentimes confused them. He had always told them that he only engaged in such apparently dirty activities to reach his objectives. His defence was that, unless he joined the dance of horror, he might not be able to clinch the governorship seat and thereby bring positive changes to bear on the lives of the citizenry. The end, therefore, should justify the means.

He never envisaged any unpleasant surprise from within the party. Yet, he did not want to leave anything to chance. The best thing, he felt, was to keep strategizing. He determined to work tirelessly as if nothing had been achieved until the day he is sworn in as governor. To this end, he hatched another plan. That night, he made a telephone call to Chief Onukwube, the state chairman of M.D.M. Both agreed to meet at Atugo. Onukwube arrived at exactly midnight and had no problem with Ebirieze's security personnel.

"My chairman, sir, I'm loyal!"

"Your Excellency," Onukwube responded anticipatorily. "I hope all is well?"

"No problem, absolutely," Ebirieze assured him.

"You know it is strange seeing the toad run on a hot sunny day," Onukwube insisted.

"Truth! my brother. But mother hen says her mission in the rains is a very important one."

"So, what is this mission that cannot wait till another day?"

"You know that a stitch in time saves nine. The delegates! It's about the state delegates."

"What about them?"

"We have to be assured of their total support. You might not be able to predict the surprises somebody may want to spring someday."

"I agree with you. The monkey said it all - that she was oblivious of the actions of the kid strapped to her back; and would only vouch for the one in her womb."

"My chairman, now you get the picture clearly. Do you know the number of delegates expected?"

"We can work that out right away. Each L.G.A. is sending six delegates. All the Executive Council members are automatically qualified. That brings the number to a figure in the neighbourhood of a hundred and twenty delegates."

"There should be something for the boys. How do we distribute packages to them?"

"I can provide the logistics. I have a list of all the L.G.A. offices throughout the state. You need to set up a team that would effectively build bridges across the network."

"Very well then! All I'd request is a comprehensive list of L.G.A. offices and officers. You leave the rest to me."

The discussion thereafter moved to other less important matters. They ate and drank until Egobuike Onukwube was ushered into one of the suites for the night. Chief Ebirieze immediately swung into action. That same week, he dispatched letters to the delegates, inviting them to a special dinner at the Okemba Continental Hotel, a popular hotel in the state capital. Ebirieze secured reservations for the delegates. He used the dinner as an avenue to appeal to them to support him in his quest for the party's gubernatorial ticket, reiterating his earlier pronouncement that he was in the race for the common good of all. Some party officers from his local government area and two neighbouring local government areas made up the organizing committee. These local government areas were Ebirieze's stronghold.

During the dinner, Ebirieze entertained questions and commentaries from delegates. At the end, it was a good investment for the chief as some of the delegates excitedly gulped down all that Ebirieze said in his flowery speech. Yet, Chief Ebirieze believed his money could always be the more effective speaker. As each man left for his room, he was given a fat brown envelope.

At the primaries, Ebirieze had little or no problems. The kernel of his speech was nothing new. The bottom line was "for the common good of all". Separately, the two other contestants spoke glowingly about Ebirieze and announced their decision to withdraw. They equally canvassed support for Ebirieze because he was, in their opinion, "eminently qualified to steer the ship of Omiemi state". Moreover, everybody believed Ebirieze had the best of intentions for the state.

Party officials at the state level had known all along that this scenario would ultimately play itself out, but some delegates were not in any way amused. To those, that was an outright betrayal by the party leadership and their so-called governorship hopefuls. A few threatened to leave the party if such was the reward they got for being loyal to the party. Unfortunately, these dissenting voices could not be heard, not even within that circle. They made up a very negligible minority. However, to Chief Ebirieze and Chief Onukwube, the state congress was very successful. They agreed that the first hurdle had been crossed. Now, their energy and resources must be channelled at the main contest with other political parties.

Who in the country is concerned about decency in political intrigues and calculations? Honesty is missing in this country's political lexicon. Genuine men of character and honour would always come out of this turf with bloodied noses. Chief Ebirieze also succeeded at effectively pocketing the leadership of the Independent Federal Electoral Bureau in the state. The state Commissioner of Police facilitated a meeting between Ebirieze and the electoral bureau's state chairman. Goodluck Aligbe, the Police Commissioner, and Egobuike had been long-standing friends in the university and the Law School. Aligbe's posting, then, was a blessing to Egobuike. It was through Aligbe that Egobuike and Ebirieze became acquainted with, and entered the good books of Alhaji Sadiq Ismaila, the state commissioner of the Independent Federal Electoral Bureau.

Ismaila was an easy-going man. A true and full-blooded Fulani, he understood the language of helping a friend, even if helping a friend meant to wilfully and brutally violate the rights of others. Ismaila had a price for help - money! Ismaila demanded that Ebirieze must be ready to part with a hundred and fifty thousand US dollars or the equivalent. The chief might also have to part with more money if the macabre dance got hotter. In Ismaila's own language, "the big men at the top shall be settled also." Other conditions included that this money must be brought in cash to a safe place where Ismaila's agent would receive it.

When the time came, Ismaila, having worked out the technicalities, sent his driver to the office of the Police Commissioner on a specified date. The money had been passed on from Ebirieze to Onukwube, and then to Aligbe. Aligbe led Ismaila's driver to his official residence and gave the driver the suitcase containing the money. For safety, the Police Commissioner assigned two armed policemen to escort the driver, with a letter for Ismaila. Neither the courier nor the escorts knew the contents of the briefcase they carried with them. This way, Ebirieze assured himself that the Independent Federal Electoral Bureau would never find reasons to disqualify him. It was also agreed that all the parties informed on this deal should work for the common good of all.

Goodluck Aligbe and Egobuike Onukwube were not left out of Ebirieze's largesse. It was little wonder then that when the review of voters' register was about to take off, the state directorate of the Independent Federal Electoral Bureau, personified in Sadiq Ismaila, duly asked Egobuike to furnish him with names of loyal party men and women who would work as supervisors and registration officers to be posted across the state.

Through radio and television, the public had been informed that the exercise, scheduled to last for a fortnight, would start daily at 8.00 am and end at 4.00 pm. In Omiemi, however, officials always arrived at the centres as late as 11.00 am. This daily late-coming notwithstanding, the exercise was deliberately slowed down to keep ordinary folks bored and frustrated. Enthusiastic citizens kept trooping out as early as 8.00 am to queue up. The majority of them were continuously disappointed on a daily basis. Following their unsuccessful bid to be registered, most of them became disenchanted with the exercise. At about 2.00 pm daily, the officials would announce that they'd closed for the day, citing a shortage of registration materials as the reason for such early closure.

This way, potentially genuine voters were disenfranchised. On the other hand, however, residencies of high-ranking officials and top members of the Masses Democratic Movement were illegally turned into alternative registration centres. These illegal centres never experienced a drought of materials. When names of party members and supporters had been exhausted, fictitious names were used to make up the lists. For the fortnight that the exercise lasted, the Independent Federal Electoral Bureau inundated the airwaves with their call to every citizen to go to the registration centre nearest to them and register. Newspapers, posters and handbills were used to complement the reach of electronic media.

The fraudulent preparations of the Masses Democratic Movement in Omiemi was not an isolated case. In almost every state of the Federal Republic of Nigeria, men and women with a perverted sense of ingenuity put such unscrupulousness to work. Different methods of electoral malpractice were devised. The leadership of several political parties took pains to "export" any such discovery from the laboratories of their Research and Development Departments to other states. They also monitored other political parties, seeking to uncover the political plans of those opponents and devising means to thwarting such plans. Interestingly, not many of them depended on the electorate to win elections. Ironically, however, no day passed without a major political campaign rally being held at one place or the other. The political climate was heating up. Close watchers of the nation's political history warned that the cloud was dark, reminiscent of the bloodbath of past years. These men were the remnants of the good old Nigerians who believed in the brotherhood of all Nigerians. However, in a country that has obviously sunk to the lowest depths of moral degeneracy, such apostolic postulations of decency and righteousness obviously portrayed the advocates and adherents as misfits. They were truly out of tune with current societal and generational trends.

Hardly a week passed without reports of political violence erupting in one part of the country or the other. It seemed to be an established norm for youth wings of various political parties and influential politicians to engage themselves in bloody battles of supremacy. Such fights witnessed free use of lethal weapons and charms prepared by witch-doctors. Casualties were recorded daily. In Omiemi, the Ebirieze Vanguard indisputably became the most dreaded political group. The high chief himself had said he believed in killing a fly with a sledgehammer. The quest for political power had brought to light all the beastly instinct and cruel disposition buried in the fleshly bodies of these politicians.

Acting true to his professed philosophy, he swiftly reacted to a potential threat to his political ambition. The governorship candidate of the Nigeria Justice Party had, in a press conference, raised an alarm to the effect that the Masses Democratic Movement had perfected plans to rig the forthcoming elections in Omiemi. He said he was indeed in possession of documents to prove this. He challenged the state directorate of the Independent Federal Electoral Bureau to publish names and addresses of all registered voters. He went further to call on the electoral body to appoint a neutral, non-partisan, career civil servant to replace Alhaji Sadiq Ismaila. Furthermore, the state chapter of the Nigeria Justice Party stated its readiness to boycott the elections if the allegations were not investigated within fourteen days from the date of the press conference.

The development unsettled the Masses Democratic Movement and Ebirieze's political machinery. Before this time, Ebirieze had believed that it was just a matter of time before he would be sworn in as the next Executive Governor of Omiemi state. He was convinced he had done enough political homework, plugging all the loopholes. He had spent money; real money! Now, who is this man who seemed bent on ruining him? What really was the vital information that Barrister Mezieihe Jideofor boasted about? Could they have stumbled on any information? Not really! Ebirieze had ensured his team members were careful enough to conceal all traces of the various underground deals he had engaged in. Was there an enemy in the camp - a mole for the Nigeria Justice Party? If yes, who could this enemy possibly be? How could he be identified and dealt with? He considered that route to be long and tortuous, and perhaps one that might not help him achieve the desired result.

If he must act, he must act swiftly and decisively. It became increasingly difficult for Ebirieze to trust men. The only ones he could feel somewhat safe around was the trio of Chief Egobuike Onukwube, Police Commissioner Goodluck Aligbe and Alhaji Sadiq Ismaila. These ones had all been taken care of. Moreover, Sadiq and Egobuike were also principal persons being accused. Further revelations might also truncate his immediate political future, if not ruin his envisioned political future altogether. He chose not to allow such a scenario to play itself out. He knew that allowing elements such as Jideofor to derail the current transition programme in Omiemi could throw up the unimaginable. His mind entertained thoughts. Finally, he called Egobuike.

"Your Excellency, sir!" Egobuike greeted him.

"My chairman! Have you heard the latest from the NJP?"

"Yes, I have! That man called Jideofor is certainly insane. How could he say such things?"

"My chairman! Can we meet at the secretariat this afternoon?"

"That's okay! What about 2.00 pm?"

"Perfectly okay! Bye!" He hung up.

Ebirieze busied his mind, browsing through possible solutions to these new problems. If those allegations were investigated, and Jideofor succeeded at proving any point, that could bring about the immediate retirement or outright dismissal of Alhaji Sadiq

Ismaila from service. If the voters' registers in Omiemi were invalidated, the Masses Democratic Movement might not be lucky enough to have their way. When they arrived at the state secretariat of the party, Ebirieze and Onukwube went into a closed-door meeting.

"What do we do about this, chief?" Onukwube asked.

"That's the very reason we are here. Think up a reasonable solution, Mr Chairman!"

"You know, this is an ill wind. If allowed to continue, it is not only capable of rubbishing our party's chances at the polls, but also affecting a whole lot of persons," Egobuike said.

"Yes, my chairman! But there's no time for analysis. The elections are just around the corner. What we need are ideas."

"What do we do with Jideofor?"

"He has to go. He is living on borrowed time."

"Yes, I agree! But how do we do this?" Onukwube asked. "You know he has two policemen officially attached to him. Again, he must have his own private security detail."

"Nothing is impossible," Ebirieze assured him.

"How do you mean?"

"Could Goodluck be trusted in this?"

"I wouldn't know. We might as well sound him out on this."

"I already called him, and he sounded very unhappy with N.J.P. and Jideofor."

"Then that's all we need. He should find a way of helping us."

"I'd ask if he could temporarily withdraw the policemen guarding Jideofor."

"But chief, that's not possible!"

"Yes, that's possible! The state Police Command should organize a one or two-day seminar for men of the force on special guard duties."

"How does that benefit us?"

"Every policeman on guard duty would be withdrawn."

"Including yours?"

"Yes, of course! That'll give us the opportunity to hit our target."

"And if Police Commissioner Aligbe declines?"

"We deploy other means."

"If Aligbe declines, he might point fingers at us as likely suspects."

"So, what do you suggest we do?"

"Why don't we go on with our plans, expunging the guard-withdrawal aspect?"

"That makes it more difficult a task."

"But not an impossible one, as you earlier remarked."

"How do you mean?"

"Policemen are human beings."

"Which means?"

"They also eat, sleep and excuse themselves for one reason or the other."

"Are you suggesting that every man has his unguarded hour?"

"Exactly! Such unguarded hour is the right time to strike."

"A close watch on the idiot for a week must yield the desired dividends."

Ebirieze decided that the matter must be handled effectively and with dispatch. In the course of the months preceding this time, one young man named Spider, a member of the Vanguard, had consistently shown himself distinctly bold and daring. His dexterity at handling weapons continued to amaze everybody. Ebirieze summoned Kololo to invite Spider to one of his guest rooms for a special briefing.

Ebirieze informed Spider that he was being sent on a special mission - that the mission would attract some handsome monetary reward. His mission was simple, he was told. He'd use a motorbike to deliver a special parcel to Barrister Mezieihe Jideofor. When he'd gone, a team of three others, led by Kololo, would closely follow him. The team would pull up a few kilometres away from the aspirant's residence and await Spider's return.

"Is that clear?" Ebirieze asked Spider.

"Yes, sir! But I have observations to make, sir."

"Yes, go ahead and make your observations."

"I am of the opinion that we should familiarize ourselves with Barrister Jideofor's residence before embarking on such an escapade."

"No! no! no! You don't need all that. I'll tell you what to do. Sit down awhile."

The chief called for some coffee as he continued.

"Spider!"

"Up chief!"

"This is money!" He doled out some banknotes to Spider.

"The state radio station has been announcing dates and venues of J.D.P.'s campaign tours. Attend one or two rallies of his and see what his security detail is like."

Chief Ebirieze stressed that if the security arrangement of Jideofor was tight, then they'd go ahead with the plan to send a letter bomb. Otherwise, outright felling of the target via a bullet at the rally would be preferred.

Three days later, Spider reported that the idea of attacking Jideofor in an open arena should be discounted immediately. He opined that based on what he saw, it would be suicidal to attempt an attack in any such rally, as the police were everywhere during each rally. The first option, therefore, remained a better approach. To further encourage Spider, Chief Ebirieze told him that upon the accomplishment of that task, Spider would be promoted to Deputy Chief Security Officer and would become the very next man to Kololo in the Vanguard. This also attracted an upward review of his fortnightly wage.

On the appointed day, the young men took off from Ebirieze's training ground at Okemba. Spider wore a coverall over a pair of denim jeans and a T-shirt. He was helmeted for the primary purpose of protecting his identity. On his hands, he wore a pair of thick gloves which seemed to complement his motorbike.

In the real sense, however, the gloves were employed to escape detection of fingerprints on any material he touched. For his defence in the unlikely event of encountering some difficulties at accomplishing his mission, he was armed with two grenades, two fully loaded 9mm berretta pistols, and a brand-new cell phone with a new line licensed to no man.

The envelope bore the logo and address of the national secretariat of the Nigeria Justice Party in Amaita district of the Federal Capital Territory, Ileole. It was addressed to Barrister Mezieihe

Jideofor with the words "URGENT AND CONFIDENTIAL" boldly printed on either side. Spider had a small hardcover exercise book that served as a register for whoever would receive the parcel to acknowledge that he duly delivered the letter. A large crowd of supporters was gathered outside Jideofor's residence. The lawyer-turned-politician was about to go to a major political rally when the parcel arrived. He handed the parcel over to his personal driver to keep in the car as he was too busy to read it immediately.

Meanwhile, Spider speedily rode back to meet Kololo and the others. Getting to the outskirts of the town, they took a turn into a dusty, lonesome road, seldom used by motorists because of its state of dilapidation. Here, they made a brief stop. The motorbike was wheeled into a nearby bush. Spider climbed into the vehicle and removed his outer garments; helmet, footwear and gloves. He dumped them on the motorbike, poured some petrol on them and set the entire lot ablaze.

A few hours afterwards, it was announced on air that Barrister Mezieihe Jideofor was dead. Details of the news were that an explosion rocked his car while he was being chauffeur-driven to a political rally scheduled to be held at Alapiti, in the eastern part of the state. His driver, police escort, the state chairman of the Nigeria Justice Party and Barrister Jideofor were all confirmed dead in the accident. There were no clues yet as to the cause of the explosion. The state police command, it was reported, had fully swung into investigation and advised everybody in the state to remain calm.

Following the death of Barrister Jideofor and his erstwhile party chairman, there were calls from all over the country for that incident to be thoroughly probed. Several theories were propounded. They ranged from assassination to black magic and sundry opinions. Chief Ebirieze was among the earliest callers on the widow of the deceased. During his visit of condolence, Ebirieze praised the virtues of the late Jideofor. He said Jideofor epitomized honesty and fair-play, and obviously would have immensely contributed to moulding a better Nigeria. Ebirieze expressed the belief that God who gave life had also taken it back, and that men should not question the wisdom of God. Unfortunately, he said, Jideofor's death would obviously take some sheen off the political landscape of Omiemi because a gladiator had passed on. Finally, he called on the police to do everything possible to unravel the cause of the deaths of Jideofor and Iroegbunam, the late chairman of the Nigeria Justice Party.

It is true that the Nigeria Justice Party hurriedly elevated the late Jideofor's running mate to become the flag-bearer of the party; the controversial issues Jideofor raised in his press conference died a natural death. The late politician's family and party were more concerned with unravelling the cause of his death and the planning of his funeral than prosecuting the case against the Independent Federal Electoral Bureau. Obviously, even if they had chosen to go on with the case, they could not have been able to achieve much. This is because the two principal parties who had access to the so-called privileged information were now dead.

A few days before the elections, the Nigeria Justice Party dramatically withdrew from the elections in Omiemi state. It directed its members and supporters to turn out en masse and cast their votes in favour of the Nigeria Moderation Party. By this act, the Nigeria Moderation Party became stronger. Being the party controlling the state government, the incumbency factor, which has always been a very strong advantage in Nigeria, would count. However, the incumbent governor also knew he faced a herculean task against the corrupt elites of Omiemi. Reasons for this were clear: the incumbent governor was a man of very frugal disposition. He believed in running a financially disciplined government, being a stickler for probity, accountability and discipline. In his bid to sanitize the rot he inherited, he stepped on several toes - so much so that some powerful cabal in and out of his party, were determined to show him the way out.

Secondly, the Nigeria Moderation Party, to which the governor belonged, was regionally strong. The south-eastern geo-political zone of Nigeria was the stronghold of the party. The Masses Democratic Movement was in control of the central government. Incidentally, both the police and the electoral body were controlled by the Federal Government. They both enjoyed little or no independence.

Often, without distinct instructions from the top, personnel of such agencies were always over-zealous to act in ways they considered to be in the interest of their masters at Ileole. By so doing, they'd not only curry their masters' favour and be certain of keeping their jobs but also of being appointed into or redeployed in more juicy offices whenever such opportunity arose. After all, in Nigeria, a historian could be appointed Minister for Aviation; a caterer - Minister of Education; and a linguist Minister of Works and Housing. It's all a matter of political leaning and patronage. Moreover, it is difficult to identify those who are truly apolitical. Civil servants are often used to prosecute the political agenda of the party in power.

Elections came. They were relatively peaceful, but for pockets of violence recorded at a few polling centres. International election observers were all over the place, monitoring the process. In Omiemi, the turnout was quite impressive. Citizens of the state chose to come out in their numbers to vote. Determined to use their franchise in demonstration of love and solidarity with the late Jideofor, as many as had duly certified voters' cards, who also suspected that Jideofor was murdered by M.D.M., voted for the incumbent. The incumbent, by reason of his splendid performance in the first four years, was eminently qualified, in his own right, to seek re-election. With the support of the teeming members of the Nigeria Justice Party, the chances of the incumbent seemed bright enough, all things being equal.

But that was only on the drawing board. In spite of the monumental voters' registration fraud perpetrated through the unholy coalition of the electoral body, the Masses Democratic Party, and Omiemi State Police Command, results trickling in from various polling centres indicated that the contest in Omiemi was a straight fight between the Nigeria Moderation Party and the Masses Democratic Party. Results were being collated as late as the early hours of Sunday morning. Agents of all participating parties went home with copies of results from their centers. Party officials and aspirants had sleepless nights adding and subtracting figures to have a clearer picture of what the results might be.

Obviously, there ought to be a run-off election between the two leading parties. Among the hierarchy of the Masses Democratic Movement, the prevalent opinion was that the new song required new dance steps. Via the phone, the foursome of Ebirieze, Onukwube, Sadiq and Aligbe chose to meet at Ebirieze's country home that night. No one among them wanted to risk going for a second ballot. They decided that figures must be falsified. Aligbe advised that such falsification must be done in a most ingenious way.

"Gentlemen!" Ebirieze addressed them. "I foresaw this situation and consequently made adequate preparations. Do not mind, we have a back-up plan."

He excused himself. Minutes later, he came back with Kololo who was carrying a tightly sealed ballot box with him. Kololo dropped this and joined Madness to fetch more. The boxes looked exactly like the ones used for the polls. Every other person was shocked. They wondered aloud how he came about those boxes.

"Alhaji!" Aligbe called, "Were you originally part of this arrangement?"

"*Walahi fa!*" Ismaila swore excitedly, "I am as shocked as you are. This chief is the number-one original crook in this country."

"We'd rather call him the number-one smart guy in town," added Egobuike.

"Gentlemen!" Ebirieze spoke. "We should not pretend as though we are ignorant of the way elections are won and lost in this country. Who among serving political office-holders in this country could effectively boast of winning elections fairly? Aligbe and Sadiq, doesn't everybody know that times like this are when you guys make your fortune? We have a gentleman's agreement that Ebirieze shall occupy Omiemi Government House this October. I have invested in this project. All I have done and will continue to do is to plug every loophole that might cause us some embarrassment.

"I hope we are all in this together. I have duly paid your prices and taken good care of everybody else. I don't expect that you all received my money secretly wishing that I would lose my stake. I believe that since we started this together, we shall work as a team until the deal is delivered."

"No problems, chief. We are only pleasantly surprised at the way you plan. You reason quite far ahead of others," Aligbe explained.

"And the fact that you got these boxes made exactly as our own boxes is another wonder," Ismaila admitted. "I never saw our own boxes until very recently."

"Well, this is proof that we are working with a very intelligent person," Onukwube noted. "Chief, this calls for some Champagne."

Ebirieze opened one of the boxes. It revealed bunches of neatly stacked, freshly scented ballot papers. With ink and pad provided, Kololo and Madness were directed to take each box to one of the suites in the complex and call as many domestic servants as they could. Those servants joined members of the Vanguard to place their thumbprint on all the ballot papers provided. The instruction was that for every ten ballot papers, six should be thumb-printed in favour of M.D.M. While the boys were doing this, Ebirieze and his three associates in fraud engaged in filling out new result sheets and forms.

Ebirieze had a trained signature expert in the complex. Joe was a brilliant young man who dropped out of school due to his parents' inability to meet up with the financial requirements of his academic pursuit. Before long, he discovered it was easy for him to decipher and replicate otherwise difficult handwriting. He then began to playfully toy with the idea of signature forgery. In time, he became a household name among advance-fee fraudsters. They gave him the alias of "Dr Brown".

It was, therefore, Dr Brown's lot to sign every signature there was to sign to do with the electoral fraud. And he did the job excellently as desired. With those documents safely handed over to Alhaji Sadiq Ismaila, the duo of Sadiq and Aligbe left before dawn. Meanwhile, there was the consensus that the ballot papers should be handed over to the O.C. Mopol for safe delivery to the Police Commissioner. Such sensitive luggage could not have had a safer means of delivery than a police truck filled with armed policemen.

Ebirieze ensured that the policemen had their fill of liquor. Traditionally barbecued beef was supplied for the khaki boys. For doing this dirty job, the policemen were also rewarded with wads of crisp banknotes neatly enclosed in clean brown envelopes. Before the police team arrived in Okemba, Ebirieze continued to monitor their movement by the effective use of his cell phone. Police Commissioner Aligbe directed the truck to the official residence of Sadiq Ismaila. It was Alhaji Sadiq's duty to interchange the contents of Ebirieze's boxes with the original I.F.E.B.'s ballot boxes.

Throughout those few days, politicians continued holding meetings, appraising and reappraising the situation. Results began to trickle in from some states. The Masses Democratic Movement was in a comfortable lead. Astonishingly, the party made curious inroads into the traditionally radical western region. The West, peopled mainly by the Yoruba, was the stronghold of the Democratic Consensus (D.C.). Everyone presumed that it would be as difficult as the proverbial passage of a camel through the eye of a needle for the Masses Democratic Movement to win a seat in Western Nigeria, but they were all dead wrong.

When the results for Omiemi were announced, Ebirieze and his team delightfully watched as those figures were churned out by Professor Briggs Winterbottom.

"In Omiemi state, the total number of registered voters was two million, two hundred and seventy-two thousand, two hundred and ninety-three. Total number of votes cast was one million, eight hundred and twenty-one thousand and twenty-five. Number of voided ballot papers was two thousand, one hundred and seven. Each party and its candidates scored as follows:

Zerennadi Uwawunkeonye of the Democratic Consensus – one thousand nine hundred and twelve votes.

Uche Ogbuehi of the People's National Party – twelve thousand, seven hundred and fifteen votes.

Okoroji Nwaugbakala of the Progressive People's Party – eighteen thousand, three hundred and twenty-nine votes.

Ogo Ezeimo of Action People – eighteen thousand nine hundred and ten votes.

Uwadimma Umunna – Nigeria Moderation Party – six hundred and two thousand, four hundred and fifty-six votes.

Sinclair Ochonkeya Ebirieze of the Masses Democratic Movement- one million, one hundred and sixty-four thousand, five hundred and ninety-six votes.

With the powers vested in me as the returning officer for Omiemi state gubernatorial election, I declare Chief (Dr) Sinclair Ochonkeya Ebirieze the winner and Governor-elect of Omiemi state. Thank you!"

CHAPTER 4.
GO SLOW

The man lay in bed. Everybody in the house was already up and going about their normal morning chores. He was rather too confused to be focused on the day. He lay in bed, not because he wanted more sleep, yet he could not rise. He had no physical weakness or disability that would impede his rising from that bed, though. That morning, what he lacked was the moral will and psychological determination to defy the multitude of problems that had arrayed themselves against him. They were all over the place, staring him in the face. He lay there, with his back on the mattress, his eyes fixedly gazing at the bottom of the decking that demarcated his floor from the one above it. He was making a mental count of the issues that obviously robbed him of his happiness. The problems seemed just too many.

It looked more like a dream but it was real. The man's situation was real. If he had not been involved, if he had not experienced all these himself, he would not have believed that all these could possibly descend on one man. In just three years! Three years!! In three years, his entire world came crashing down. His experience within those years could only be summed up by the word "nightmare". It is the type of nightmare that one would immediately wish to come out of. But then, wishes were no horses. Life is unpredictable. He wondered if God ever existed. If God were in existence, would he really have allowed all these? Does this God not see the hearts and know the constitution of every man before assigning roles to them in the drama of life? Why does this God choose to impose such psychologically wrecking roles on him? That is if God really existed.

The man continued on this super-highway of mental monologue. There were too many questions that needed answers. If only this God could be located. Oh! If this God could be seen, then the man would be among the very first to consult him; the first to go directly to him and demand explanations for the myriad of problems buffeting him. But this God seemed so far away. So far away! Those preachers on television always talked about the nearness of God. In fact, they always declared that God is with men. However, the man was yet to see or hear of any who physically encountered this God. Even his next-door neighbours had always been carried away and driven to frenzied ecstasy by the finesse and words of those men of God. Many a time, the excitement and rather ostentatious display of religious bigotry had been carried too far, too far into his very own rights' zone. He never quite understood them. He remembered that when these folks lost their only son, their grief was very brief. They had consoled themselves in the belief that the deceased was resting in the bosom of their Lord. The man concluded that such a manner of thinking was the product of warped minds.

Solutions to the man's problems seemed too far-fetched. Every day, the man continued to sink deeper and deeper into the horrifying abyss of despair. The man had died, that is, in spirit. Though he lived and walked the earth, his spirit was long gone. He was no longer enthusiastic about life. The burdens of life were so heavy that he was overwhelmed by them.

Though he managed to hang on, the very fabric of his life was continually being eroded by the brutality of those forces. The coalition of forces, he reasoned, had been rather too intimidating. Part of its inextricable complexity was the fact that those forces were not visible. Had they been visible, he certainly would have asked to know why they had chosen him as their successive host? He remembered that only a few years ago, there was the sweet aroma of wealth all around him - the very fragrance of comfort. Just about everybody in his extended family courted his friendship. He remembered how generous he had been to everyone, family or not. He possessed a generous heart but lacked the material equivalent of that heart to match his will with action. Incidentally, his troubled mind, humiliated by the current predicament, felt no longer qualified to think of itself as being generous. The issue at hand was the search for a means of freedom from the combined grip of these terrific enemies.

The man suddenly remembered that the landlord was scheduled for a visit that day. There were times when he was indifferent to the landlord's visit. In those days, he was doing well financially. Then, he was any landlord's delight. Today, however, the storm of life has eclipsed the former success story. For the second year running, he was yet to pay his rent. The estate agent had written severally to him. The first was to remind him that his tenancy was due for renewal. Thereafter came the one mildly demanding explanation for his failure to meet his financial obligations to the agent. Then meetings! It was after the second meeting that the estate agent, Olumide, expressly called the man's integrity into question. Olumide had flippantly remarked that the man was deliberately withholding the rent. The man's explanations to Olumide that the entire workforce of the Nigeria Fertilizer Corporation was owed salaries of over eighteen months' duration only seemed to infuriate Olumide.

During that visit, Olumide had told the man that the economic downturn being experienced in the country was a national malaise and was not limited to only one man. He questioned the rationale behind the man's confessed inability to pay his rent when the man and his family were subsisting. Olumide drew the man's attention to the fact that the estate agency business was his own means of subsistence, and that the man should be able to raise money through whichever means possible to meet his tenancy obligations, just as he had been doing for the daily upkeep of himself and family.

The man stood with his mouth agape, petrified by the shock that the young estate agent could throw decorum to the winds in such a manner. If anything, the man was not prepared for this because he just could not believe that this once courteous son of O'dua could descend so low as to challenge an elderly man with such causticity, questioning the man's very integrity. It was well over five minutes before the man recovered from the shock and diplomatically reminded Olumide that he should not lose his long-held African value of respect for the elderly, even in the face of provocation. In very civil and non-offensive language, he tried to drum the message home to Olumide that hardship could be experienced by anybody at any point in time and should not be viewed as the special rights or privileges of any man or group.

The estate agent viewed this from rather a different perspective. He concluded that the man was not being realistic. He told the man that the African in him was no reason for him to become timid and unwilling to let his tenants know the true state of things. According to him, he would be failing in his duty if he could not convince tenants to pay their rent. Other estate agents, he said, could also scheme him out of the management of that property. When that happens, then the foolishness of such emotionalism and the so-called African values would be revealed.

The man sighed as he turned over in bed, now lying on his stomach. With his hands supporting his chin, he rested his elbows on his pillow while continuing that morning review of his apportioned lot in life. Today, the immediate problem was the expected visit of his landlord, Engr. Okebata. Nigerian landlords! He had heard so much about the inconsiderate way landlords treated tenants in Lagos. Prior to this time, he had not experienced any such treatment. A few years back, he could have bet any amount of money that he'd never experience the wrath of Lagos landlords. He had acquired a piece of land in a choice Lekki Peninsular neighbourhood and was fast developing it when fate dealt him a blow. He then instructed his engineer to temporarily suspend work on the site. He did not know that he'd never add another stone from that date. It was not to be until he sold the property for a little above half the amount he had sunk into that project.

Today, he regretted the decision to sell the property in the first place. He believed he was ill-advised. Probably, his family might have managed to survive. The money from the sale of the property was split into many parts and used to take care of such things as school requirements of the children, the rent for that year, and other sundry matters. The bulk of it was deposited in the bank while the man prepared for the launch of his new business outfit. The biblical Job syndrome which seemed to accompany the man reared its head here also.

His bank got enmeshed in that terminal financial disease called distress. Hanavas bank used to pride itself as the *"commercial bank to beat"*. The man was not privileged to be pre-informed of distress signals in the bank. If he had an insider in the bank, he could have known quite early. At first, he did not want to believe that his deposit was lost. That position was predicated on the claims made by Hanavas bank management that their bank was never distressed. They had headed for the courts to prove that the hammer of the National Deposit Insurance Bureau was illegally applied and politically motivated. Citing deposits in excess of fifty-two billion naira, an asset base of over ten billion naira, and shareholders' fund of close to thirty billion naira, they wondered how a bank with such intimidating evidence of stability and buoyancy could be termed distressed.

As the bank went to court, the man hoped there'd be some light at the end of the tunnel. He hoped against hope, until hope gave way to doubt, and doubt equally caved in to despondency. Today, the decision to deposit his fund in that bank continues to haunt him.

Certainly, he thought, something must be wrong with this country. Is it really that something is wrong? Nothing is right. This is one country where everything is wrong. Every right thing has been bastardized. A man should not dare to keep huge sums of money at his residence. If one decides to do so, the chances are very high that cockroaches, geckoes, and mice who cohabit with him would inform armed bandits that there's money in the apartment. If such money is eventually stolen, the whole gamut of blame and righteous indignation shall be directed at the supposed fool whose money was stolen. Ironically, when one shows himself informed and avails himself of the services of a bank, the story of distress comes with its accompanying headache. So, why this country?

The metal gate leading into the compound opened with a creaking sound. The man turned in his bed and sat up, surveying the gate area from the vantage position of his bedroom window.

"Oh no," he muttered, "the landlord has arrived at last". So early? The man wondered. Ordinarily, the man was of a sound mind. He was considered healthy and very courageous. Under normal circumstances, no man could ever count him among the cowardly. But lack and deprivation have a way of cutting a man to size. The man's inability to meet his financial obligations had reduced him. He had long lost his voice among men. In the company of the landlord were his wife and Olumide, the estate agent. The man knew there was some trouble in the air. He got into the lavatory, washed his hands and his face, and went into his room again. Osemudiahmeh, his third daughter knocked on the door and informed him that Engr. Okebata had come. The man walked to the sitting room to welcome these dreaded visitors.

"Good morning, lady and gentlemen!" He greeted them in his impeccable English accent. "Good morning, sir!" they all responded. Olumide stood up and began to speak.

"Sir, we have given you enough time to pay your outstanding rent. Our decision is to recover the flat from you and put it to some other use. Here is a letter to that effect!" he said as he handed a letter to the man. The man cleared his throat and stood up to plead for more time, promising to pay as soon as he receives money from any source. Unfortunately, nobody wanted to give him that benefit of the doubt. They only showed contemptuous indifference to whatever he had to say. The landlord also orally delivered part of the message contained in that letter. He began, "Mr what is he called? I did not come to Lagos for charity. You do not even know how I laboured for the money with which I built this house. You know I am a Christian and would not want to lie to you. The truth is that the apartment in which I currently live is not my property. The owner has also asked me to leave. You know the place too well. I live in a duplex. This place you currently occupy is a three-bedroom apartment. I and my family would have to put up with it until the man occupying the detached bungalow moves. We intend to give him notice to quit also. So, the issue is not really centred on your inability or unwillingness to pay. Even if you issue a cheque for a three-year tenancy now, I wouldn't accept the money because we need this place. God bless you!" With those words, the trio left.

The man thought about this. Oh no! Engr. Okebata needs this place. Well, he opened the letter and saw some other reasons. In the letter, the estate agent had asked the man to vacate the apartment within one month of the receipt of the said letter because the landlord has special but urgent need of the apartment. Attached to this letter was a copy of the letter from the landlord, instructing Olumide to serve the man notice to quit. In the letter written by the landlord, he claimed that his eldest son, Saka would soon be getting married, and would move into the apartment.

Furthermore, he authorized Olumide to set in motion the machinery for the legal option, should the man prove stubborn. A copy of the letter was also made available to his solicitor. The landlord's words that morning contradicted the message expressed in the letter. The only place of agreement between both was the opinion that the man should vacate the flat. Otherwise, the landlord was not being honest. This was not funny. Okebata and Olumide had some other things in common. Besides the management of this property, both were very strong and committed members of a Christian ministry whose international headquarters is situated in Gbagada, Lagos.

They were evangelicals who had always been involved in the business of taking their Lord Jesus Christ to the world. What on earth could make them invent such lies? Obviously, they were lying. The man had seen through them. First, the landlord said about his family moving into the man's apartment. Now the letter reads that the first son would need the place. Who on earth told them that he had no intention to pay? Well, he concluded that neither Okebata nor Olumide should share any blame. They were human after all, he reasoned. But it left a sour taste in his mouth that men whom he had respected all those years for their continued tenacious hold on their faith were the same men who were now proving themselves unworthy, just because of their unfounded suspicion of him being dishonest.

It equally amazed him that both men, being persons with whom he was closely acquainted for over eleven years, could change their perception of him because of the few years of hardship he was experiencing. He was not a Christian. That is, not a zealous, church-going Christian such as Olumide and Okebata. But for the sake of decency, he believed men should be fair to one another. His disappointment was based not so much on the fact that they asked him to move out, as much as the dishonest fabrications they were using to achieve their desire. He remembered the popular saying of the lizard that "she was not angry with the man who passed the death sentence on her, but that her real anger was boiling against the one who said she should be flung to death". The latter proposed an inglorious, dehumanizing method of dying for her.

"Honey! what is it?" the man's wife asked as she came in.

"A quit notice! They have given us notice to quit within a month or they'll take some legal action against us," he told his wife.

"It's good for you! Are they not the same people you took as your very own? Every Christmas you'd send them hampers. Whenever you travelled out of the country, you'd bring gifts along for them."

"Sweetie! Why do you speak like this?" the man asked. "Would you equate hampers and sundry gifts with a two-year tenancy of a three-bedroom apartment with its appurtenances?"

"All I am saying is that they have hit you below the belt. They don't know anything about fairness." The woman insisted, "If it were you, you'd never send your tenant packing for such reasons as this."

"Human beings are not the same. We have different faces. Our temperaments and perceptions may also differ. The only thing I don't understand is why Okebata refused to believe that I'd pay him."

"Why should he believe?" the wife asked. "Don't you see that his so-called estate agent, Olumide has brainwashed him with negative images of you?"

"Leave the young man alone. He has a family to take care of. I understand his wife is expecting another baby soon. Besides, they already have four kids. The wife is not employed, you know."

"So, is it your money that Olumide is waiting for to take care of his family? If you do not pay, then his children would die of starvation and his wife in childbirth eh?" the wife asked again.

"You don't understand. The young man has no other means of livelihood. Moreover, he's afraid that Engr. Okebata may ask him to withdraw his services. Olumide does not want to lose the management of this property."

"Okay! It boils down to the same thing; money! Everybody serves money in this country. In any case, where do you intend us to move to? Don't other tenants in this place pay? What about Prince Isaac - the man who occupies the bungalow? Is he also owing? And the Diepriye family! Are they owing? Sincerely, I do not understand what your plans really are. What exactly do you want us to do?"

"The landlord says he wants to move into this place. Why should I prevent him from doing that?" the man asked.

"The property belongs to him," he continued, "and I definitely have no powers to deny him the use of something legally owned by him. In the meantime, we'll think of what to do."

He stood up, stretched himself, and got back to the room. While in the room, the man yawned. He was hungry. The previous evening, he went to bed without really having dinner. The dinner of rice prepared was rather too small to serve everybody in the house. He had simply told his wife and children that he was not hungry. Throughout the night, he'd sleep and wake up in turns. The hunger pangs he had made him feel as though he hadn't eaten for three days. As dawn approached, he slept briefly and woke up to the reality of the landlord's visit. Now, the landlord had come and gone. He reasoned that he must not starve himself to death. Thank goodness that Oyawu brought some beans home that morning. Oyawu, the man's second son, worked at Ogba. He'd go to work every evening and work all night long. He was a casual staff member of a drug manufacturing concern. His immediate younger sister, Eromosele was a teacher in a privately owned nursery school at Thomas Salako Street, Ogba. From their residence in Haruna Street, Ifako, Agege, they often trekked to their places of work.

This Saturday morning, Oyawu had bought some beans on his way back from work. The quantity was large enough to serve the whole family four times. The man's children had begun to adjust to the new realities of life. They all tried to brace themselves for the new challenges. The idea of using faggots as domestic fuel was not in any way pleasant; not with the characteristic smoke that pollutes the immediate environment. Moreover, it was not easy for a family that had all along enjoyed the benefit of electric and gas cookers to embrace the use of faggots. From electric and gas, they moved lower to the use of kerosene stoves. Now faggots and charcoal were the common fuel. Kerosene was only used sparingly, whenever some extra naira notes found their way into the family purse.

The man had sold off much of what he owned. Besides the cookers, the family had sold two cars - a Mercedes Benz C-class and a Toyota Landcruiser V8 four-wheel drive. The only car left to serve the family was a 1990 Model Peugeot 504 S.R. The Peugeot had deteriorated so much that the main frame looked more like jagged pieces of metal haphazardly welded together. It created an image of disunity and incoherence. It no longer underwent routine servicing. Originally, there was a Toyota Camry reserved for the children's use. The Camry was damaged in an accident before the man's current predicament began to unfold. The Camry was wasting away in the morgue of the mechanic's village, awaiting a final requiem mass from the man's family.

Most of the electronic gadgets that served the family had also been sold. All that was left included an old Sony colour television, A 1979 JVC radio/cassette/recorder, and a Philips twelve-band world receiver transistor. No item could be considered of luxurious importance any longer. Though every stakeholder in that family was beginning to adjust to those conditions thrown up by uncertainties, one issue that continued to jag at the man's emotional and mental essence was Nosa's case. Nosa, the man's first son had been a thorn in the flesh.

He was a Law student at the University of Ibadan. One fateful Monday evening, he came home with his bag and baggage. Every member of the family was surprised and wondered what the matter was. The surprise was not at seeing Nosa in the house not quite a week after he had left for school, but the rather bizarre attitude of the young man as he came back. He had come with virtually every piece of property he owned - items of clothing, electronics, mini gas stove, boxes, bags and plates. In fact, he came back with everything he owned in school. Alarmed, the man asked Nosa why he had come home the way he did. The young man only replied that he was tired of the school and could not continue in such a hostile environment.

That was considered a rather strange answer. It was barely five months before his degree examinations. The man asked to know what kind of hostility the young man was talking about, wondering why such a hostile environment had not existed in the past four years. This January, everybody in the family contributed all they could to ensure Nosa went back to school. Every family member looked on Nosa's education as top priority. They had built up hope around him, not only because he was the first son, but also because he was studying to become a lawyer.

That night, the man decided to find a means of fuelling his car the next day. He was determined, notwithstanding the risk involved, to drive all the way to Ibadan. He wanted to find out the reason behind his son's sudden loss of interest in his academic pursuit. However, that trip had to be indefinitely shelved, since every piece of information the man needed was made available to him during the national news on television that evening. According to the news broadcast, three students were confirmed dead, and fifteen others seriously wounded in a bloody clash between members of rival cults in the university community. The university authorities had acted very swiftly and called in the police who made some arrests. Some of the suspected cult members made useful statements to the police. Consequently, some dreaded members of those cults were now at large and had been declared wanted by the police. Nosa's picture appeared against his name. When Nosa's name was announced, his mother collapsed out of shock but was later resuscitated. Throughout the broadcast, Nosa locked himself up in the boys' room. Even after the broadcast, he refused to see anybody and threatened to commit suicide if pestered further.

Early the following morning, the man drove to Area G. Police station at Ogba. He made a report that his son's name was announced as one of the wanted cult members in relation to the Ibadan killing. He requested that some policemen go with him to effect the arrest of Nosa. That was done. Ever since then, Nosa and some of his fellow student cultists have been in detention. For over eleven calendar months, the Police had been unable to properly arraign them for prosecution, claiming that investigations were yet to be concluded. A battle erupted in the man's mind. Was it proper for him to have given Nosa up as he did? But wouldn't he be doing more harm than good to society and himself if he had accommodated Nosa?

Wouldn't he be an accomplice to their crime if he had pretended not to have known about the disgraceful and wicked act? Yes! Nosa must abide by the consequences of his actions. No man deserves to live who takes pleasure in snuffing life out of another. The law must be allowed to take its course. That morning, he mentally gave a second approval to the way he handled Nosa's case. He also decided not to go and visit Nosa for anything. The fact that he had been brought low by problems was enough reason to say he could not afford the expenses of going to Abuja every now and then. The transfer of the suspects to Abuja, therefore, was a blessing in disguise.

But looking at the issue again, he bemoaned his fate. Life, he felt, had not been fair to him. If problems and difficulties in life were to be shared equally among the living, he believed that all he was experiencing was enough for three individuals. He felt he had more than his fair share of life's afflictions. In as much as he approved of his action regarding Nosa, he invariably felt sorrowful that his first son might never come back to him again. Nosa was the beginning of his strength. He did his very best to bring Nosa up in honesty and civility. He had been providing for himself and his family in all honesty. Though he loved the good things of life, he never went out of his way to attain them. He never really believed in joining the rat race of the acquisitive society in which he found himself.

The Toyota Landcruiser he once owned had been a gift from men who had been privileged to gain from his honest disposition. He had championed their rights as workers with the Nigeria Fertilizer Corporation and turned down all the baits dangled before him by the core Management. For him, it was his normal altruistic self in service. At the end, the group honoured him with that car on his birthday.

As for the Mercedes, he bought that when he came back from a training course in the United States. He had saved much in those six months, as his salary was being paid monthly in Nigeria while his allowances in hard currency were just more than enough for him. Besides, he bought the car from a Dutch national - a colleague who had been recently retired and was going back to his native land. The price was unbelievable; a real give-away!

The man's frugality reflected in virtually everything he did. When it came to food, his habits were abstemious. So how did Nosa get himself enmeshed in the shame that is called cultism? Young Nosa had always cut the picture of a gentleman of the finest breed. He was always particular about his appearance; a real stickler for excellence in public mannerisms! In the family, he was everybody's darling. Easy going and humble, nobody who knew him in Lagos would suspect that Nosa could ever belong in a cult. On the façade, he never hurt a fly. Handsome, intelligent and always clean-shaven, Nosa was soft-spoken. He had some charm about him that meant just everybody would easily take a liking to him. How then could such angelic physical features house such a wicked spirit?

The man seldom spoke. Nowadays, he chose to speak only when he considered it necessary. Yet his mind was being overworked with thoughts. People around him thought he was trying to bear his misfortune with equanimity. More than that, he was only pining over the avalanche of troubles. This new trouble of being asked to move out within one month provided a fresh source of worry. The landlord had asked him not to pay what he was owing though, but what would he do about his family?

Was it easy to secure an apartment in Lagos even when a man had some money? Without a farthing, where would he consider the starting point? The message from the landlord that morning was bad news. The man already owed neighbours here and there. His blood relations seldom helped. None of those relations ever visited him again. Oftentimes, when he visited them, he'd notice strange movements, and then somebody would come out to announce that the man of the house was not at home.

His kin had abandoned him. Those were people he never failed to assist whenever he was approached for one form of assistance or the other. Today, they no longer remembered him. He bore his cross alone. A few friends were willing to help, but they were not in such a financially buoyant state as to be of any meaningful help. Occasionally, those friends would come bringing some foodstuff with them. They'd bring *garri*, rice, beans, tubers of yam and beverages. If not for those ones, who knows how rough it would have been? It was rough already, but it would have become unimaginably rougher.

"Daddy! Food is ready," Osemudiahmen announced as she brought in a plateful of beans porridge on a tray. For the past month, the family menu had been rotating between beans porridge, rice and eba. Rice in this context is not prepared in the popular Nigerian style of jollof, fried or white rice with stew. Rice for the man's family was always cooked with red palm oil, salt and pepper. Onion and other spices were optional, depending on their availability. Fish or meat of any type was completely ruled out of rice dishes. No food was reserved for a particular mealtime. They are taken as they come. If the family woke up in the morning and confirmed the availability of *garri*, then they'd prepare *eba* with any type of soup and eat.

They had managed to sustain the use of what they called meat in making soup for *eba*, courtesy of the man's wife. When she was forced to go to the market at dusk on a certain day, she saw sizeable heaps of bones and cartilage on the tables of some butchers. These obviously did not appeal to most buyers. The man's wife was able to buy some for a sum she considered paltry. When they were cooked, it was obvious that even a well-fed dog might protest at being served with some of these.

When Osemudiahmen served the man, it was about eleven o'clock that morning. Everybody knew that after brunch, the next meal would be in the evening. Before he set out to eat, the man called his wife. She was a middle-aged woman, tall and slim, but the configuration of her teeth was rather unusual. One canine tooth on either divide of her dental outlay was disproportionately projected, disrupting the otherwise smoothness of that dental arrangement. Her skin was lustrous ebony. Her hair, a mixture of black and silvery grey, looked clean and charming. A mother of seven surviving children, she was now in her late forties, but she looked more like a young woman of twenty-eight. Seeing her daughters stand side by side with her, no man should be blamed if he called them her siblings.

She had borne all those troubles along with her husband until this day. The landlord had come with this frightening possibility of ejection within a month. Her feminine spirit, resilient though it was, had reached that elastic limit of endurance. As she walked to the dining table to answer her husband, her mind, made vacuous with the shock of the impending doom, could still not reason properly.

"Sweetie, sit down!" he said, "let's discuss as we eat". He stood up, held her hand and helped her to a seat.

"I have an idea," he continued. "I'd go to the village and sell my own portion of our late father's land."

"How could you think of such a thing?" she asked. "Have you considered the children? Where would they build in the future?"

"It is only a man who is alive today that may think of tomorrow," he answered. "However, we may sell a portion of it for us to start life all over again."

"Well, if you insist. It may later turn out to be the best decision now," she concurred.

"Perhaps we shall pick up our bits from there."

That evening, the man trekked miles to the house of a cousin. The lady, now married and experiencing an upward trend in life, obviously enjoyed some financial prosperity. The couple lived at Dideolu Court, a middle-class residential estate in Ogba Ijaiye. As he trekked, he was in two minds. Jane, his cousin was not always forthcoming when approached for help. He thought of Jane at this time. He wouldn't sincerely wish to go to Jane again, but circumstances were compelling him to go. He could swear that Jane was the most niggardly creature that ever lived. She was niggardly whenever she eventually chose to give. Oftentimes, she'd table a thousand and one reasons why she could not give. During the man's travails these three years, he had come very close to outright rejection of Jane's miserly gifts. Those numbers of times also, he had managed to rule his own spirit. He would then receive those things offered with a grin, muttering some expression of gratitude, while feeling great pain and insult within.

This time, Jane received him warmly, offering to bring some food. The man turned down the offer of food, and quickly let Jane into the details of all that had transpired in his apartment that morning.

"So, what exactly do you intend to do now?"

"That's the reason I came," he answered. "I need some money to travel to the village. Probably, I'd be lucky enough to dispose of some parcel of land. At the worst, the family could get a new lease of life from there. I'd pay it back as soon as I could."

"When do you wish to travel?"

"If you could assist me with the money, I'd leave Lagos first thing in the morning."

"Tomorrow?"

"Yes! Tomorrow."

"Well, I really empathize with you. However, the suddenness of your plan makes it impossible to part with any money now. When asking for money, you should give somebody one or two weeks' notice to get the money ready. Things are generally bad in this country. I feel your pains but every farthing I have now has been earmarked for a specific project, and my husband would not find it funny to hear that I diverted money to other causes without his consent."

"Could I speak with him, then? I'll talk to him personally," the man requested.

"Oh no! He's very tired. Besides, I do not want to upset him with any request for money. He's just come back from Abuja, and I doubt if he has any dime left in his pockets."

"So, you mean to say you can't give me anything?" the man asked again.

"If it were possible for me, I would have done so. What I told you is the true situation of things. Never mind, though, it will soon be over. All these problems shall come to an end sometime, and very soon for that matter," she consoled.

"Okay, sister. Bye-bye."

"No! Hold on please."

She went into their bedroom and thereafter came out with her husband. Seeing this, hope began to rise in the man. He thought there had been a change of mind. He exchanged greetings with Charles, Jane's husband. Jane touched the man's left hand, and with her own right hand transferred some notes into his palm, then added voice to it. "At least you could use this for a bike ride to your house."

"Thank you!" the man muttered, managing a smile as he turned to leave.

Charles decided to walk down the road with him. That was intended to be a mark of honour. The man could not resist the temptation of bringing up the issue again. When he did, Charles corroborated his wife's position while commiserating with the man. Charles was philosophical in his approach. He told the man that though he was passing through some tough test, the latter part of the man's life would likely be very rich. He enjoined the man to be happy, contented and grateful for life and all its benefits.

"Consider our situation," Charles said. "Everybody thinks we swim in an ocean of money. Perhaps they believe we have some goldmine somewhere. Sincerely speaking, I'd modestly say we are comfortable. But I'd trade all that comfort for what you have: four grown-up girls and two boys, Nosa's detention notwithstanding. You are abundantly blessed. Could you just think of us for once? We've been married for twenty years and are without a child. The story might have been different if we had children and lost them. We have always prayed to God for children, yet none has come. My wife, your sister does not know what a woman feels when a baby kicks in the womb. That's our portion of life's misfortune. We do not run from pillar to post bemoaning our situation.

"Besides, you may not know the responsibilities I shoulder. I currently train six undergraduates. My nieces and nephews all depend on me. My aged parents live on my support. If my only brother cannot afford to bear the financial responsibility of training his children in school, do you think he could effectively take care of my parents? All that he does in the village is to take a share of whatever money or material I send to my parents. That is the true position. Now, do not get the message wrong! We would have loved to assist, but rendering such assistance is practically impossible at a time like this. You may have to try elsewhere. Surely, you intend to pay back immediately you arrive in Lagos.

"I'll go back from here. Have a very pleasant trip to the village. Do let us know when you come back," Charles informed him, bidding the man goodbye.

"Thank you!" the man said, not encouraged to say more.

His mind raced down to a family who'd been one of the few pillars of support to his family. They were the nearest kith he could approach that evening. Again, he was not happy going to them. His unwillingness this time stemmed from the fact that these ones were only managing to subsist on their meagre wages. Moreover, they had done beyond the man's expectations. Every month, with religious regularity and faithfulness, they came with money and foodstuffs. With two children, they lived in a two-room apartment, sharing a common kitchen and conveniences with other tenants in the yard. To go and talk of money again was to overstretch this family. They had done more than their ability.

But he had to go. Otherwise, he might not travel. He was not credit-worthy. There's no friend or relation who was ignorant of his condition. As many of them as he could reach had earlier been reached at other times. When a man goes to borrow, tradition demands that he'd fix a definite period of repayment. How would he fix a time of repayment when he did not even know the next time money would come into his pockets?

He trudged on, depressed in spirit, angered in his mind, and tired in the body. He walked spiritlessly to Ijaiye road, took the left turn and dragged his weak body to the Ogba bus stop. There, he caught a bus to Ojodu-Berger. At the Grammar School bus stop, he quickly alighted and was about to cross to the other side of the road when the bus conductor called out to him, reminding him that he had not paid his bus fare.

"I'm sorry!" he said, giving him a twenty naira note out of the hundred naira that was tucked into his shirt pocket.

Being too tired to trek the distance, he finally crossed over to the other side of the road and boarded a motorbike to Oremeta Street. It was already past nine o'clock that evening when he pressed the doorbell. At first, he was almost deceived by the absence of his friend's car - deceived into believing that his friend was not at home. Little Glory came and opened the door. She stooped in typical Yoruba tradition to greet the man.

"How are you, Glory?"

"Fine, sir! You are welcome."

"Is Daddy at home?"

"Yes! He's watching the television. Do come in and sit down, sir."

"Good evening Toyin!" the man greeted his friend.

"Thank goodness I met you."

"You are welcome, sir! I hope all is well?" Mr Toyin Illofa asked, surprised at the visit of his friend at such an odd hour.

"Sit down and let them get you a drink," he offered.

"No, thanks! May I see you outside for a moment?" the man requested.

"Yes, of course," Mr Illofa obliged as they walked out of the door into a common passage.

"We have been ordered to quit our apartment," the man began.

"Ah! Oluwa wa o!" Toyin exclaimed. "Don't say that, please."

"I have tried in vain to raise money to travel to the village. In all honesty, I did not wish to come and bother you. However, it has come to the point where you are the one person I can always take as a brother."

"How much do you need?"

"Anything you can afford; any amount that can take me to the village and bring me back."

"Today in this house, we have only eight thousand naira earmarked for my mother. The money is still with us only because we are yet to see someone trustworthy enough by whom it would get to Mama. What do you do?"

"I understand," the man said, believing this hope was equally dashed. "I have to go, sir."

"Let me confer with my wife first. Please come in and give us two minutes."

Toyin called his wife into the room. A few minutes later, he came out and announced their decision to the man, handing an envelope over to him.

"This is all the money in this house today. Use part of it to travel and keep the remaining with the family. It is eight thousand naira."

"My goodness!" The man exclaimed. "All this? I promise to pay it back as soon as I sell that parcel of land," he added.

"Not to worry. We are not expecting it back."

"So, what about your old mother?"

"We'll see what we can do before the new week runs out."

"Thank you, my brother. You really mean so much to me. I'll have to leave because it is getting late."

"Cheers! Have a safe journey to the village."

With the money safely in his pocket, the man heaved a sigh of relief. He regretted ever going to Charles and Jane. He wondered why he did not go straight to Toyin Illofa instead of cheapening himself before his cousin and her husband. All the same, he was glad. He could tell that when tomorrow comes, all things being equal, he would travel to the village. He had no call credit in his mobile phone. Metropolitan Ogba was still very busy at this time of the night. He stopped over at a call centre and made a call through to one of his subordinates.

The following day being Monday, he arrived in his village, set within a sleepy countryside with undulating little hills and valleys, and a network of ponds and rivulets. It looked more like a ghost town since most able-bodied men and women had migrated to the big cities in search of better means of livelihood. The rest had gone to the farms, markets or about some other businesses. The man's aged mother and some domestic animals were present to welcome him home. Initially, the old woman was oblivious of her son's presence. She was busy cracking palm kernels, which she was intending to combine with some tapioca for lunch. Sitting on a short wooden stool, she had wrapped up her lower body with a piece of old, faded Nigerian wax. Her upper body was bare, revealing a pair of sagging flabby breasts. Her face and skin were heavily wrinkled, like an artistic masterpiece of a network very visible to the ordinary eyes. Her hair, brownish grey in colour, was unkempt.

"Mama!" the man called in an emotion-laden voice. At the sound of that voice, a pregnant she-goat lifted its head and bleated. The old woman turned and simultaneously rose from her seat. As she stood to walk, she was bowed over and used a wooden staff to aid her movement. Her old, shrivelled face brightened up at the sight of her son. When she smiled and welcomed him, she exposed the current state of her mouth. Her teeth, now brownish from an age-long use of raw tobacco, openly declared they were mourning the loss of half a dozen members of their kindred. The man quickly dropped his hand luggage and embraced his mother.

"How are you, my son?" she asked. Not waiting for an answer, she added, "I am well informed on the state of things with you. Don't you worry, eh! All will be well."

"Mama, who is telling you all these things?"

"Am I not your mother? When the going was good, I know how you always provided for me. I am grateful to Oritsha that I am alive and that you and your family are all alive and well."

"Mama, I am sorry. You have suffered much. You don't look healthy," the man said, now sobbing because he had been unable to take proper care of his mother as had been his practice.

"Where is Agadia?"

"He left for the King's market in the morning. He'll soon be back."

"What about his wife and children?"

"They all went to the farm. The children have not gone to school for the past week because your brother has not paid their school fees."

He brought out a loaf of bread from a carrier bag and gave it to his mother. He went into the general lounge, dropped his luggage and brought out a long wooden bench which he placed beside his mother's sitting position. He sat beside the old woman and placed his right arm on her shoulder, in a demonstration of affection.

"Mama!" he called again. "It is my responsibility to take care of you. I know I have failed you. I ask for your forgiveness."

"What have you done wrong? Are you *Oritsha* who regulates the affairs of men?"

"No, Mama! But I ought to be able to take care of you and save you from this humiliation and hardship. It is my fault."

"I am alive, my son," the woman assured him. "The determination of the spirit to live is the elixir that keeps the body alive. Don't you see that deprivation and lack do not really bring about death?"

"My son," she continued. "Troubles of the mind - heartaches and worries, they are the real causes of death."

'No, Mama! You don't understand. It is an indictment on me that I cannot fulfil my obligations to you."

"Spare yourself some trouble, son. Take it easy with life. Tomorrow is pregnant."

Then the man's younger brother appeared. Agadia! Grotesque in appearance! Broad-faced! Bold-toothed! He wore an afro hairstyle, the fashion prevalent some fifty years earlier. Agadia was seven inches taller than the man. His hair was rough and poorly kept. His eyes were planted in deep hollow sockets, and his head stood on broad masculine shoulders. His biceps impressively bulged out, cutting an image of a world wrestling champion. Those biceps would intimidate any challenger. His thighs were well developed, proportionate to those biceps. He strode home with a gracious gait, like a lion king that had just eaten his fill of fresh meat.

The muscles of his unsmiling face further contracted as a result of his long time standing at the market. He'd been there trying to sell off a few he-goats and roosters he took to the market. The day was almost gone when he sold off the last one. He was quite surprised at seeing the man in the village. If he expected anybody, surely not this brother whom he had long counted as lost to the city.

"Greetings, Agadia!"

"Welcome brother! How is Lagos?" Agadia responded.

"Things are rough, my brother," the man said. "That's the reason I'm here."

"How is everybody over there?" Agadia asked further. "What about your wife and your children?"

"They all send their greetings. Everybody is alive and well."

Dusk was approaching when Agadia's wife and children came back from the farm. Home-reared fowls and goats found their way back in pairs and groups. Before long, Agadia's wife had prepared a local delicacy of starch with *banga* soup. The dish was rich in bush meat, fish and local spices. Everybody ate to his satisfaction. After the meal, both men were served with a keg of fresh palm wine. It was customary that serious matters were discussed under such conditions.

"My brother," the man began, "things are pretty difficult for us. These are very trying times for the family."

"It is no different here," Agadia stated. "I wonder what this country is turning to. We were told that all they do at Abuja is to sit down and agree on the formula to share government money among themselves."

"We had better think of ourselves first. Abuja is too far from me today," the man stated.

"So, what is it that brings you down here this time?" Agadia asked.

"Eh em! It is that land - that piece of land. I intend to sell a part of it - a part of what belongs to me, really!" Those words stung Agadia like the attack of a female bee, provoking fury in him.

"How dare you think of such a thing?"

"No, Agadia. You don't understand. I'm talking of my own share of our father's land."

"For your information, you don't own a square inch of that land anymore."

"What did you just say?"

"I have taken legal possession of that land."

"How do you mean?"

"That is to say that the documents all bear my name."

"Who says?"

"You probably need more information. I have leased out eighty percent of it for ten years. I have also picked up the cheque and paid it into my account at Ughelli. I am currently awaiting the clearance of that cheque."

"How could you do such a thing without informing me?"

"Father trained you in school. He gave you a good education at our expense," referring to himself and their sisters.

"So, what does that imply?"

"Your education is the property he bequeathed to you. You are educated. You belong in the city."

"Agadia, what stopped you from acquiring education?"

"Your schoolmates are professors, federal ministers, advisers and highly placed technocrats in various fields today. All you could think of is to come home for the sole purpose of selling off your father's property. Shameless city man."

"Agadia! What has come over you?"

"Nothing!"

"Are you insane or what?"

"On the contrary, I have only chosen to be reasonable this once."

"Does being reasonable mean taking over what belongs to both of us?"

"I advise you to stop prying into this issue any longer."

"I don't understand. Is that a threat?"

"This is to enable both of us to live long enough to accomplish our goals in life," Agadia threatened. There was a murderous, sullen look in his eyes.

"Agadia!"

"I advise you to leave for Lagos as the cock crows. You do not belong here."

"We shall see to that very soon."

Back in Lagos, the man was driving to the office in his old rickety but faithful Peugeot 504 saloon. On a good day, driving from College Road, Ifako to Ebutte-Meta could easily be accomplished in an hour and fifteen minutes. However, a traffic jam, which is a regular phenomenon at different parts of the metropolis, oftentimes elongated such trips to two hours and more. This morning, the man's vehicle crawled past Ogba, Acme Road, Adeniyi Jones Avenue, Aromire Road, Allen Avenue, Opebi Road, and was at Mobolaji Bank in Anthony Way when the traffic situation became unbearable for him.

Traffic wardens were stationed at the junction linking Ikeja Country Club (almost opposite Eko Hospital) and Mobolaji Bank - Anthony Way. These traffic wardens had obviously lost control due to the uncaring attitude of road users. Everybody, just everybody wanted to have the right of way at the same time. Vehicles in their fleets streamed in from three different directions. Like soldier ants from all corners racing instinctively towards a mass of decaying oily food, men behind those steering wheels seemed very eager to score first in the centripetal movement towards Maryland bus stop.

This attitude, rather than facilitate movement, was an impediment to the free flow of traffic. Frustrations increased. Horns blasted. The man could hear people swearing and cursing.

"Ole ni!"
"Olori buruku!"
"Weree!"
"Don't hit my car o!
"Madam's driver!"
"No be that license you buy?"

It was horrific! It was so bad that the lengthiest single movement any car made was about three meters forward. In the confusion, a screen replaying events of the past weeks invaded the man's mind. They pricked at his emotional essence. In quick succession, his mind went berserk, visiting different scenes and personalities at a rather supersonic speed. These harried him. He remembered his brother Agadia. He remembered the current state of his family. He remembered the quit notice issued by Okebata and Olumide. He remembered his children. His wife. His mother. Nosa, his son. Oh no! Problems! He felt some sharp pain on the left side of his chest. Then again; he tried to breathe. He discovered he was panting...difficult gasping. He choked. Then he escaped. He escaped the troubles of this world.

It was time to move again. The old metallic grey Peugeot 504 did not move. Its engine revved, yet it was stationary. Those behind the Peugeot ceaselessly blared their horns, vainly anticipating that the car would move. Minutes afterwards, the driver of the vehicle immediately behind the car of the deceased came out, fuming with anger.

"*Oga wetin dey happen now?*"

No response.

"Ah-ah! Are you sleeping on the steering wheel? *Yeye man! Wetin you dey do for night wey you no fit sleep? Abeg move your car joo!*"

No response.

He moved closer and pushed the head which was rested on the steering wheel. The arms drooped. He pushed further and was jolted at what he saw.

"The man is dead o!" he screamed and quickly dashed away, farther from the man's car.

"What did you say?" a lady who had just emerged from another car asked.

"The man is dead! He's as dead as a dead man could possibly be," the Volkswagen Golf driver reaffirmed.

"Why not call the police, any hospital, the emergency services, or arrange to take him to any nearby hospital?" the woman suggested.

"What?" the Golf driver asked. "Do you want to get me in trouble?"

"How do you mean?"

"I am not ready to answer ceaseless questions about things I do not know. Moreover, I don't want to report late to the office and incur the wrath of my boss." With those words, he boarded his car and tried to manoeuvre his way out of the traffic jam.

CHAPTER 5.
ENTRY RESTRICTED

Alhaji Dauda was a very influential man. In Michika, he was a beacon of light in the twin fields of politics and investment. He was a member of the board of directors of several blue-chip companies. He was the chairman of a few others. His vast financial empire and political clout notwithstanding, he chose to permanently reside in rusty and rural Michika. With modern communication facilities at his disposal, he perfectly managed his affairs on all fronts. In the neighbourhood where he lived, he was held in awe as a strict disciplinarian and father to everyone. He had four wives, as was permitted by the creed of his religion. That was his current status. The number of his wives exceeded twelve if one should count former wives whom he had sent packing for one excuse or the other.

A septuagenarian, his natural strength was like that of a sturdy stallion. In addition to his everyday menu, he ate roots. There were different roots he identified as health supplements. These roots were very efficacious in doing whatever Alhaji intended them to do. Alhaji seldom used modern toothpaste and brush to clean his teeth. His preferred choice was a local chewing stick. He believed that the chewing stick was not only effective at cleansing the teeth but was also medicinal and potent enough to strengthen the gums and freshen the mouth.

His youngest wife, Salamatu, was barely eighteen and was just out of secondary school. She was an epitome of *Higi beauty* in this community in Adamawa state of North-eastern Nigeria. Dauda's homestead was a large one. There were close to twenty different houses in that compound. The high fence created a very good sense of security for its inhabitants. His family was equally large, comprising eighteen male and twelve female children, not including those who had moved into their own homes, and the girls who had been given out in marriage. The retinue of his domestic servants numbered over fifteen. Surprisingly, he had no officially hired security man. There were over a dozen men who worked voluntarily as guards and gatekeepers for Alhaji.

On the door of each of the apartments of his wives, there was an inscription: *baa shiga*, which meant that visitors, especially men, were prohibited from entering the rooms. There was a large and centrally located lounge in the main house. This generally served the purpose of a sitting room. Italian marble of the finest quality covered the entire floor of the lounge. This lounge was modestly furnished, yet the furniture bore witness that Dauda was not only a man of means but also a man of exquisite taste. Due to the rather high traffic of visitors to that house, it became increasingly difficult for this lounge to successfully satisfy everybody's requirements in the area of reception of visitors. Alhaji extended the privilege of using that lounge to all members of his household, primarily to keep an eye on those visiting.

The immediate frontage of Alhaji Dauda's house was even busier than the lounge. Twice a day, with religious regularity, Dauda fed close to a hundred persons in this open space. Street urchins, the poor, and the destitute were assured of some meal at Dauda's expense. These included some blind persons and some whose limbs had been chopped off because of crimes they committed in the past. No matter how hungry a man was, he surely would find some food for his stomach at Dauda's place. On a good evening, the scene resembled an evening market in Southern Nigeria.

In the very spirit of reciprocity, no man who has been fed from Dauda's hand would either speak ill of him or join forces with his enemies to fight him in any battle. It was not that Alhaji Dauda was grooming them to fight his battles, but that they all saw him as their benefactor. He was truly the big daddy. When decisions on national, state or local matters were to be taken, these men and women, along with their families, colleagues, and friends, would always defer to Dauda. They often aligned with whatever position he took. Alhaji Dauda was convinced that the allegiance of these men was more than the faithfulness of an Alsatian. To him, these men made up his extended family.

His political stature was equally colossal. For forty years, he had been the undisputed godfather; the real strongman of Gongola politics. His sphere of influence was wide. It was so wide that almost thirty years after the creation of Adamawa and Taraba out of the former Gongola State, he continued to wield enormous influence, not only in Adamawa but also in neighbouring Taraba. Every politician seeking an elective office in both states always consulted him. Without Dauda's blessings, that political venture would most certainly be aborted. Whenever he fully threw his weight behind any politician, however, the task before such a politician was made easier. He was the number-one political gladiator of Nigeria's north-eastern geo-political zone.

Candidly, in this country, the saying that "nothing goes for nothing" is an enduring truth. The consultations these politicians made with Dauda included agreements on the following areas: the amount of money needed to sponsor a candidate (in the event of those seeking his sponsorship) and the percentage of interest payable; the expected level of patronage accruable to Alhaji when his candidate eventually succeeded; and a firm promise on oath that the status quo would be maintained as long as the aspirant would be in office.

Dauda's wives were strictly prohibited from making an unauthorized public appearance. They must show themselves decent enough and committed to the tenets of their religion on womanhood. In the unlikely event of any of them appearing in public, her entire body must be decently covered. Her outward appearance must strictly conform to the acceptable norm as outlined in the written code. This was because Alhaji believed that inner purity must also reflect on the outward appearance. He held the teachings of the prophet sacrosanct. The entire Michika community extended the respect and admiration they had for Dauda to his wives.

Young Salamatu had a problem with this, but she could not privately confide in her husband, let alone openly confess to others. The teenager in her was roaring to join the bandwagon of youthful exuberance. Her wedding had been arranged without her full consent. Though Alhaji Dauda was well-respected and seemed to be the dream husband of some young ladies, he was apparently forced on Salamatu. Days before the wedding, she had gone to visit her friends. No sooner had she entered than her friends began to happily greet her with the traditional greetings meant for a new bride.

"Amaria, sannu nki de awure!" Kudirat enthused, smiling infectiously.

"How is your sweetheart?" Halima asked. "How lucky you are! While some of us are trying to think of what next to do with our lives, your wedding is only a few days away."

"Please spare me the trouble! Who says I am in a celebration mood?" Salamatu warned.

"Me ya faru? What is the problem?" Rabi asked.

"Is it that none of you sees anything wrong about it—that at my age, I should go ahead and marry a seventy-year-old man?" Salamatu asked.

"Is he not better than these young boys who come running after us?" Halima retorted. "They cannot even buy themselves a good pair of trousers, unless one uncle or the other spares them some money."

"Do you mind, Salamatu?" Kudirat added. "I wish I could swap places with you. Just give me old Alhaji and everything he has, and take Isiaku, my juvenile playboy for whatever you want to do with him."

"He could be yours for the asking, Kudirat. I sincerely don't know why I should go into this marriage if not for the insistence of my parents."

"That's very correct, Salamatu," Rabi answered with some sarcasm. "Wise parents know exactly what is good for their intransigent daughters."

"What's that supposed to mean?" Salamatu asked.

"That daddy and mummy made the right choice." The three girls sang.

"Okay girls! Could we please get more serious about this?" Salamatu appealed, looking helpless.

"That's true!" Kudirat concurred, showing some serious concern about the matter. "If it is happening to one of us today, it surely could happen to another tomorrow."

"I think you're right, Salamatu. Poor girl! I empathize with you," Halima agreed. "These parents of ours don't want to move with the times. They are forever battling against every wind of change. I'm afraid that someday, change will sweep their feet off the ground," she added.

"That's the thing I'm saying. I wish I could just stand before my father and coerce him into consenting to the opinion that I will not marry Alhaji Dauda, that pot-bellied old man," Salamatu said, clenching her right fist.

"But you would do exactly that, wouldn't you?" Halima dared her. "Go ahead; do it and damn the consequences."

"Sincerely speaking, that's an area that I have not summoned enough courage to tread on," Salamatu said, confessing her weakness.

"That means you have chosen to die in silence." Rabi judged. "I have only one life, and I must live it for myself. Nobody would dare live it for me," she said assertively, beating her chest with her right hand for emphasis.

"You all know my father. I have already approached him and let him know my opinion. But I'm afraid; it made little or no difference. He's really crazy about tradition and religion," Salamatu said, further betraying her helplessness.

"That's the very thing that has kept us backward and underdeveloped for ages. Tradition! Tradition must be dynamic for it to foster love, understanding, and unity," Rabi said, bringing in a bit of philosophy.

"Be careful girls!" Kudirat counselled. "Tradition is a very strong force in our part of the world. Our people may not just understand if we suddenly begin to resist it. Tradition distinguishes us as a people."

"That's why our growth is stunted," Halima added, toeing the same line as Rabi. "We place inhibitions on ourselves and later blame others for our woes. Countries of the world have constitutions and provisions for amending these constitutions. These traditions and culture make up our local community constitution. Why don't we ever amend them?" she asked no one in particular.

"Have you seen Mustapha?" Rabi asked Salamatu, introducing another dimension. Mustapha was the young male friend of Salamatu.

"No, I have not. I called him several times on the phone, but he just wouldn't answer my calls," Salamatu responded. "I wonder why everyone is behaving strange and funny these days?"

"I met him yesterday," Rabi informed her. "He accused us of misleading you."

"Does he think I have no opinion of my own?" Salamatu asked.

"He also claimed that you betrayed him by reneging on your promise to marry him," Rabi continued.

"That's it!" said Salamatu. "Everybody knows I did not renege. It's unfortunate that Mustapha himself does not appreciate the pains I'm being made to go through in all this. But the problem I have with him is that he's unreachable. If he'd sit down and listen to me, he'd probably help me with wise counsel."

"That's the truth," Rabi agreed. "He is avoiding every one of us as if we are leprous."

"I think he is beginning to behave like one of these old men who hold on to an opinion and never want to change their minds," Kudirat judged.

"Leave the poor boy alone," Halima said, defending Mustapha. "He's only sulking over what I'd rather call the violent tearing away of one part of him. His heart must currently be bleeding because he is deeply wounded."

"Is that enough reason for him to suddenly abandon me at this time of my travail?" Salamatu asked. "Whose wound is bigger, his or mine?" she added.

"I believe he has not demonstrated enough courage," Rabi opined.

"No! I rather think he believes he could easily switch to another girl as soon as he chooses to," Kudirat suggested. "Basically, the kid goat learns how to chew palm frond by carefully observing the practice of its mother. He's learning to act like the older men of this same stock."

"What do you call the girl-child born in this part of the world?"

Salamatu asked. "Are we not more or less their domestic animals?" she added.

"We are slaves to men of culture and tradition," Rabi quipped. "The most annoying thing about all of this is that there's hardly any difference between the educated and the uneducated among them," she added.

"Neither is there any difference between the young and the old," Kudirat agreed.

"Be patient, girls! We shall be free someday." Halima spoke with a tinge of prophecy.

"Only the heavens know how long it would take us to crawl into that state of freedom. Perhaps the fourth generation of our offspring shall see it," Salamatu said as she left the girls.

Salamatu wondered how her father could nurse the idea of letting a man old enough to be his own father marry his daughter. When the plan to give her in marriage to Alhaji was made known to her, she had earlier expressed her disapproval of such to Amina, her mother. But her mother had strictly rebuked her, warning that she should never mention such a thing to anyone else. Her mother had told her that what was important was the fact that Alhaji was a man of considerable wealth: that her daily bread and that of her children yet to be born were assured. Amina equally reminded Salamatu that Alhaji Dauda was very committed to his religion, their religion. Salamatu did not give up. She had persisted with her plans to let her parents know her position. She had approached her father on the issue.

"Baba na!" she called as Musa was resting in an armchair under a tree. "Do you remember that proverb - that the hen said her reason for shouting was not for her captor to free her, but that the world may hear

her? I know your mind is made up on this, but I'd like to make my point clear."

"And what is that point, if I may ask?"

"That I am now beginning to wonder if you really love me."

"Why do you nurse such devil-inspired thought in your mind?"

"Because I find it difficult to believe that you care for me in the face of this apparent rape of my freedom."

"Did I hear you say a rape of your freedom?"

"You heard right, Baba! I feel terrible! I feel like a worthless piece of garbage. I am only one among other pieces of garbage littering your house. If you treat me this way, you'll soon pick up other pieces and throw them away as you intend to dispose of me soon."

"It is not exactly so, my daughter. We must promote our culture and not discard the tradition of the elders. We embraced these practices. They have been working for us. They worked for generations of our forebears. They shall also work for you and your children."

"Baba, shouldn't a woman have a say on an issue that may affect her for a lifetime?"

"When did children in Michika begin to dictate to their parents on the issues of matrimony?" Musa responded with a question. "Besides, it would be a total disgrace and disappointment if it happens otherwise, considering my position in the religious cum cultural tradition in Higiland," he added.

"I knew you'd never see anything wrong with it, so far as it is called tradition! Today, you have decided to slaughter my lifetime's happiness on the altar of your inconsiderate and rigid tradition."

"Dan iska! Wahali talahi," he swore, 'I know that you want to become a useless child. But I want to tell you one thing: that by the will of *Allah*, I, Musa Mamoud, would not be alive to see you marry one useless riffraff or infidel. I shall not sit down and watch you drag the family name in the mud."

"Do as it will please you. But I have a piece of advice for you: that whatever I become tomorrow; you should be bold enough to let everybody know that you chose that path for me. Good evening, *Baba!"*

That night, Salamatu was troubled. That was before she visited her friends. She had been dreaming of going to the university to study medicine and surgery, and then proceed to specialize in neurology. Now, that dream seems to be evaporating into the thin air. Her father's decision would most likely change the entire course of her life. It came all too sudden. There was hardly any time to hatch a redemption plan. Running away could provide some temporary relief. However, she could not think of anywhere she would run to. Most of her kith and kin were ardent believers, sharing the same religious philosophy as her father. Moreover, she was aware that if she ventured an escape and failed, misery would be added to her woes. Based on these, she stopped every form of complaint, choosing to wait until she got to her new home before thinking up another plan.

That night, she went to bed bewailing her future life of confinement and solitude. She was well-informed that at the time, Alhaji Dauda had three wives. She knew that Alhaji's third wife, Aisha, was a very educated woman. She was the one everybody knew as Alhaji's wife. She was always publicly seen with Alhaji Dauda. Anytime he had a social function to attend, Aisha would always be by his side. It was common knowledge that Alhaji regarded the other two women as old and worn out. They only seemed to adorn the house because their children were grown and wielded some influence. Several other women, in the name of wives, had come and gone. Some left very ingloriously. Some left without bearing any child for Alhaji. But Aisha was there, like the rock of Gibraltar.

Somehow, Salamatu felt she would be no different from the other women whom Alhaji had married and later dumped. Moreover, she was apprehensive that Alhaji was rather too old for her, and might as well join his ancestors soon, thereby making her a young widow.

At her age, she was just metamorphosing from girlhood to womanhood. Now, she felt like a mango fruit, ripening and mature enough to attract the careful eyes of humans, and possibly to help to satiate the appetite of one. She knew she could not really refer to Alhaji as her own. He would be a jointly shared commodity, with Aisha taking the lion's share, and leaving the remnants for her and the other wives and mistresses to divide between them. And who knows, Alhaji might well be planning to acquire more wives, as he seemed to be obsessed with the acquisition of women.

When the day arrived for Mallam Musa to formally give his daughter's hand to Alhaji Dauda in marriage, it provoked different emotions in different individuals. While Musa was proudly happy that his daughter was getting married, and that he might become a grandfather soon afterwards, young Salamatu was melancholic, as though she was mourning one part of her. Her spirit was heavy. Her father's words kept ringing in her mind. Tradition! It was the tradition of the elders. They had embraced it that way, and nobody was doing anything to change it, even if not totally wiping it away. "Oh!" she exclaimed. "Tradition should have a human face, and not be a monster to terrorize humanity."

When she was called out for the traditional bridal dance, her eyes were like twin fountains, pouring forth endless streams of tears. She tried to wipe those tears, and shrug off the mood, but to no avail. Her close friends continued to dab her eyes with handkerchiefs. They truly empathized with her, and demonstrated camaraderie, contributing their little attempts to soothe her sorrows. She managed to dance to the rhythm of the music, but rather exhibited the most inconsistent steps ever imagined. Guests misinterpreted this, thinking it was the emotional turn quite common with young brides- that she was already beginning to have an advanced feeling of nostalgia.

Another song jolted her out of that depth of despair. She smiled to herself. People around her applauded, thinking she was pleased with the turn of events. That song was the favourite song of Rhoda, her classmate and friend. Rhoda was a Christian. Whenever Rhoda felt melancholic, she'd withdraw herself and begin to sing:

Nobody knows the trouble I've seen. Nobody knows but Jesus.

Not my papa, not my mama.

Nobody knows but Jesus.

Not my brother, not my sister. Nobody knows but Jesus.

Strangely, Salamatu was shocked to know that she could sing that song. For her, it had been a Christian song all the while. She never really made the effort to learn how to sing that song. In her family, Christian practices were strictly forbidden. On this day of her wedding, however, that song just sprang up from the inner recesses of her mind. Now she could tell why Rhoda always sang that song. It truly made some sense now. It was that both her mother and father did not care, or that they did not understand the torture they were putting her through. Only Allah would understand her plight. And maybe, Rhoda's Jesus also, she presumed.

That night, a train of well-wishers accompanied her to her new home. She was awed at the splendour and symmetry of the internal arrangement of her new home. Alhaji Dauda had tastefully furnished a two-bedroom flat for Salamatu. She was immediately ushered into this. Here, she'd begin a new phase of her life. Celebrations continued at the compound till dawn. In the morning, she woke up with her husband beside her in the bed. Just as she was wishing him good morning, her mobile phone rang. While she was trying to yawn and fight the residue of sleep that lingered in her eyes, Alhaji stretched his right arm across Salamatu and picked the handset.

"Hello!" he said. "Salamatu will call you as soon as she rises from the bed. Thank you." He still held on to the phone.

"Who was that?" Salamatu asked.

"I don't know," he said. "I only informed that you'd call back. I think you still need some rest."

"Oh yes!" she said softly and tenderly. "But I thought it would have been more proper for me to take that call," she suggested.

Still holding on to the phone, he pressed the menu button and scrolled down to call records. Then he got to received calls. As soon as the name of the caller was being displayed, he extended the phone closer to Salamatu's eyes, intending for her to see the identity of the caller.

"Oh!" Salamatu exclaimed. "Kudirat is such a darling. She must have called to find out how I am adjusting to my new home. I should call her immediately. Do you think otherwise?"

"I have no problem with that, but just hold on for a moment."

He stood up and walked to the wardrobe, opened it and brought out a pack containing the latest iPhone handset. Then he picked out a new mobile sim pack. Walking back to the bedside, he said, "Your old phone ceases to be yours from today. You may give it out if you want to. However, the line is being effectively withdrawn from today. That's a better handset." He gave the iPhone to her.

"And a new line," he added as he also gave her the sim pack.

"As part of the grand design of taking possession, and to ensure that my lovebird is not unnecessarily bothered with unsolicited calls, we'll delete a number of names from this old line. Only the names we'll jointly approve of shall be transferred to the new line. This is to forestall any situation that might pose some threat and embarrassment to the family."

"But all the names I have in that phone are names of family members and friends I personally relate with," she protested.

"Not to worry, dearie, we'll see to it that you don't lose contact with your very close acquaintances. We'll screen the names together," he assured.

Alhaji did exactly as he promised. But for the names of Mallam Musa Mamoud and Salamatu's male siblings, Dauda ensured that all male names and the female names he was not comfortable with were deleted. Salamatu didn't quite understand the rationale behind that decision. To her, what was beginning to unfold was confirmatory that her initial fears were real. She never imagined that her own husband would suddenly try to cut her links with as many friends and relations as he chose. Her worst nightmare was never close to anything like that. She then imagined the possibilities that could rear their heads in the weeks and months ahead.

The entire arrangement had seemed rather stupid to her. She had been bluntly told by her father that she should not have an opinion on whom to marry. She also did not have the privilege of getting properly acquainted with the so-called suitor before the marriage. Everybody who considered himself wise and informed averred that it was normal practice; and because it was normal, it was assumed good. Obviously, she felt she was with a stranger in that bed. Yet, she couldn't do a thing to free herself. She felt like a trapped bird - a bird put in a cage to provide pleasure and amusement for some humans.

Then she began to inwardly examine her mind. She was trying to get some inner assurance that she had not lost her sanity. She probed deep into her mind. Was she weird? Why does almost everybody have a different opinion from her own? The only ones who shared her views were her three friends. But their opinion was considered inconsequential. They were yet considered suckling in matters of religion and culture. But she was convinced that they really meant well for her. Kudirat's early morning telephone call confirmed that her love and affection were not affected. They were real. The other real fact was that she was married to Alhaji Dauda and must try as much as she could to adjust to life as his wife.

She was only seventeen years old at the time of her wedding ceremony. A few weeks after joining Alhaji's harem, Salamatu became quite confused. She almost began to nurse the idea that her parents were right after all. This was because Alhaji began to shower much love on her - much more than she could ever remember anybody else giving to her. Her first year in her new home was like a dream world, a real paradise. That very first week, Alhaji took her on a shopping spree. He bought several new dresses, skirt suits, trouser suits, different footwear, sashes, make-up, fragrances, and textile materials to be tailored to Salamatu's size and style.

He ensured that she discarded all the garments with which she came from her father's house.

Besides the provision of these material things which money could buy, Alhaji specifically detailed three domestic servants to primarily attend Salamatu. Among these servants were two women and a man. The man was to act as chauffeur to Salamatu whenever she needed to go out. The ladies were to do her laundry, cook her food, run her errands, and engage in other domestic chores Salamatu might have for them. There was a Honda Accord car specially reserved for her. Personally, Alhaji Dauda showed himself to be a very affectionate man.

He was caring. The wonderful thing about him was not about what he provided, but more about his personal profiles of gentleness, love, and care. He was a very good listener. When he listened, he always seemed to be emotionally involved. He also took time to answer every question as satisfactorily as he could. His sense of humour was rather extravagant. Whenever he was with Salamatu, he created an atmosphere of hilarity and peace that would surely linger beyond that communion. At times when Salamatu took ill or felt feverish, Alhaji would treat her like a baby. He would pamper her and literarily spoon-feed her. He retained a very brilliant physician as the family doctor. Her new home was an entirely different world from the one in which she was raised.

Whenever Dauda was out of town, he would call Salamatu a dozen times on the phone, getting first-hand reports on the state of her wellbeing. She was always sure of a new gift from him whenever he returned from his numerous business and political trips. Most members of the family rather relied on Salamatu, not only to get information on Alhaji Dauda's movement but also to get their benefactor to fix one personal problem or the other for them. Concomitantly, everybody in the family extended some form of loving care and friendship to Salamatu. She really was in her element and felt she had the world at her beck and call. She was the newest bride.

The change in her status was quite phenomenal. At social functions, minstrels always sang her praise. Her friends of yesteryear began to see her as a type of economic Messiah. They often asked for her assistance to solve some minor financial problems. Several times, however, she wouldn't wait for them to ask before she'd give help. Alhaji apparently gave to her without asking her to give an account of how she spent the money. She effectively touched the lives of her parents and siblings in a very noticeable way. Whenever she was coming into or going out of Alhaji's house, tens of the less privileged who fed at Alhaji's house would bow before her. She symbolized the reigning queen of the estate.

A few times, Alhaji took his young bride on trips in and outside the state. Steadily, he began to introduce her to some of his friends and associates. Within six months, Salamatu had not only totally adjusted to life in Alhaji's home, but she also became obsessed with his love. Alhaji Dauda reigned in her life. He lived in her thoughts. He lived in her revelations and dreams. He lived in her real world. He conquered. She became convinced that her parents were right. She was grateful to Allah that she was dragged into this marriage. Her confessions changed. While with her parents or friends, she did not fail to sing the praises of her husband. In his presence, she would always say, *"miji na, ina kauna ka ai"*, meaning, "my husband, I truly love you". That was her own way of professing her love for her heartthrob.

But Salamatu was dead wrong. It was not yet freedom for her. After one full year of that marriage, things began to change. Gradually, the average time she spent with Alhaji dropped considerably. Sometimes, she wouldn't be able to see her husband for an entire day, even when he was in the house. He'd travel and spend some days without calling her on her mobile phone. When she eventually called him, he might choose not to answer that call, or assign somebody else to answer, who would inform her that Alhaji was in a very important meeting. When he came back home, he'd reprimand her, accusing her of monitoring his movements. He'd remind her that she was not his only wife, that he had other wives and that he considered himself strong enough to marry many more wives if he chose to.

Salamatu began to wonder. Grief and weeping became her companions. She couldn't really pinpoint what the problem was. She did not really have a problem with Alhaji. If they had a quarrel, she knew that Alhaji, in his characteristic way, would call her and resolve it. She scored him highly in the area of communication. He was a master at that. But she needed her husband to be by her always. She needed a companion, a friend with whom she could share the issues of life.

Though Alhaji was yet wonderful at providing for her and other members of the family, provision of such material things just couldn't fill the gap of a human companion. She also realized that as Alhaji steadily withdrew from her, other members of Alhaji's household who hitherto had courted her friendship began to trail the path of their benefactor. The only ones that continued in their loyalty were the three personal aides. However, even these ones were not as friendly as they used to be. They continued to carry out their domestic duties, ensuring that she never lacked help on that front, but they became much more formal. They gradually reduced verbal communication that was beyond their domestic responsibilities. She noticed this, but in her wisdom chose not to ask questions yet. She was convinced it was a true reflection of the position of the family head.

In the early hours of a certain Friday morning, Alhaji invited Salamatu to his bedroom for what he called "a very crucial discussion". During the discussion, he told her that it was now one full year since he married her. "I gave you all the love and attention you deserved for that first year of our marriage. You could bear me witness that I deprived others to make you happy. *Koba haka ba?"*

"Haka ni," she agreed, wondering what Alhaji was up to currently.

"There is a time for everything," he continued. "You must have noticed that I no longer give you as much attention as before."

"Yes!" Salamatu said. "What went wrong?" she asked, sitting up and brightening up her face in anticipation of an answer.

"Nothing is wrong. Certainly nothing!" he assured. "I believe you are well acquainted with the provisions of our religion on marriage. You were entitled to one year of undivided loyalty. Moreover, it was my own way of making you feel happy and welcome in my household. However, just as I said earlier, the time has come for me to review everything."

"What happens next?" Salamatu asked, afraid that she was yet a stranger to Alhaji. She discovered she was wrong to have mistaken all the care, attention, and provision of material things for real love and marital bliss.

"You remain my wife, and my newest bride for that matter, but you may no longer continue to enjoy those exclusive privileges and perks."

"Why?"

"Simply because justice must not only be done but must be seen to have been done. I must not give preferential treatment to any one of you."

Dauda thereafter informed her that the honeymoon was over, though the marriage continued. He specifically told her that her position was now like that of the others, and that he had invited her to let her know what is expected of her in the new dispensation. He encouraged her to be strong for herself, as she was no longer considered a girl, but a woman.

"This does not mean that you are loved less, but that all are loved equally."

He said that and dictated the code of conduct.

"From today," he said, "note the following:

You are officially wife number four.

In the interest of everybody, you must always stay indoors.

You must obtain my express permission before you leave the premises.

In the event of number three (3) above, you must not leave unaccompanied.

On no occasion must a male visitor be spotted in your apartment.

You are free to visit my room, but only at my invitation.

A list of your monthly personal needs must be passed through Hajia Aisha five days before the end of every month."

He paused and looked at her. She held her two hands together, partly resting her chin on them. Her right forefinger was vertically projected across her lips as if she was warning herself not to utter more words. Alhaji Dauda himself was not new to such. He had seen different women react in different ways to similar situations in the past. He wanted to end that dialogue fast, so he chose to throw a question at Salamatu.

"Do you have any questions?" he asked.

She took a deep breath in, breathed out, and shook her head, indicating that she did not wish to ask any question.

"I still love you," he told her, holding her hands and giving her a kiss.

Salamatu left that room more confused than she was before she entered. Her initial confusion arose from her ignorance of the reason for Alhaji's sudden change towards her. Now she was let into that reason. The reason for her confusion changed. It was now about the propriety or otherwise of that marital relationship. It was like a dream - a wild dream. She could imagine what the future held for her. She was married yet might now really begin to live like a single woman. Now that Alhaji Dauda had unequivocally told her in no uncertain terms, what the future most likely held for her, she decided to brace herself to the challenges and fight for her happiness.

"A man rejected by others does not reject himself," she soliloquized. In a bid to fight boredom, and to rekindle the flame of fellowship among her former circle of friends, Salamatu began to burn more credit on her mobile phone, spending much more than she would normally spend. She needed to re-establish old links severed by her husband during the early days of her marriage. Only her trusted friend Kudirat could perfectly do that job. Communicating with her old friends was her own way of trying to make herself happy. She was determined to revive her social life. For her, that social life had experienced swings. It was on the ebb. However, with Kudirat, she was sure of fanning the sleepy hearth into a burning flame again.

She soon acquired a new mobile phone, successfully ensuring that Alhaji was totally unaware of that. Rule number one for that phone was that it never rang. Nobody called her on it. Rather, she made only a few calls from it. Secondly, when she called anyone, her number was always hidden. Thirdly, she preferred to send and receive short messages via that phone. Finally, it was always switched off. It was switched on only when she needed to use it, and that was always when Alhaji was out of the house. Soon, she was able to get linked up with Mustapha again. She was discreet enough not to attract suspicion. Via the phone, Salamatu took time to explain issues to Mustapha. She finally convinced him not only that she was forced into that marriage, but also that she still loved him.

Mustapha himself seemed to have acquired some new zest and was determined to recover what he felt was rightly his. He believed Salamatu was cruelly stolen with the collaboration of hard-line traditionalists. His spirit was charged like that of a lion robbed of its cub. But they could not see each other yet. They were barred by circumstances created by other humans. Consequently, both began to explore possible avenues through which they could physically meet.

This continued for several weeks. Salamatu was assured of hearing Mustapha's voice several times every day. She was comforted. Salamatu wanted something beyond hearing Mustapha's voice on the phone. She longed to see him. However, she knew it would take much more intelligent planning and careful execution to physically see him. She was now very well known in the community. Besides, she was warned by Alhaji not to leave the home unaccompanied. Though her aides were no longer as close to her as they used to be, they remained steadfast at doing what they were detailed to do. By extension, she knew she was under very close observation. She couldn't possibly keep an appointment with Mustapha outside her home.

With the co-operation of Kudirat, Salamatu's dream became real on a Friday afternoon. Having feigned illness three days earlier, she found enough reason not to attend the *jumat* prayers of that day. Mustapha and Kudirat had contrived a plan. Mustapha shaved himself clean. With the help of Kudirat, Mustapha effectively disguised himself to look like a young woman. His body was totally covered, head to toe. This was permissible for a category of brides. He appeared like a new bride under restriction. Both visited Salamatu. Since Kudirat was the only friend of Salamatu who had earned the trust of Dauda, the visitors had no problems getting beyond the gate and the general lounge. It was customary to visit the sick.

Not too long after they arrived, Kudirat excused herself. She said she had some urgent matters to attend to and promised to come back soon. Salamatu and Mustapha were, therefore, left alone. That time offered them more opportunity to explain issues and their former positions in clearer terms than they could do on the telephone. They were still discussing, carried away with the excitement of such a reunion, when Danladi, the driver, overheard them, recognising the voice of a man. He walked closer to Salamatu's door and stood there to convince himself that he had heard right. When he confirmed his suspicions, he ran to Alhaji Dauda's private apartment to relay the news.

"What stupid joke are you trying to play?" Alhaji Dauda asked, not willing to believe the report.

"Alhaji!" Danladi said. "I am telling the truth, the whole truth, and nothing but the truth. With my very ears, I overheard him," he swore, affirming that his report was factual.

Alhaji Dauda sprang to his feet, dashing directly to Salamatu's flat. He banged at the door with such ferocity that it sent chills down the spines of the two discussants.

"Open this door immediately!" he ordered.

Salamatu opened the door. The gentleman turned woman sat on the sofa, with his entire body neatly covered, perfectly acting like the woman she pretended to be.

"Is there any problem, my lord?" Salamatu asked.

Dauda was dumbfounded. He looked rather stupid.

"Who is this?" he asked, pointing at the female figure in religious attire.

"Meet my friend Mariam. She came visiting with Kudirat this morning."

"Salam maleku!" Mustapha greeted him in a tiny little voice, in conformity to the female image he bore.

"Maleku salam!" Dauda responded. Turning to Salamatu, he asked, "who else is in this flat?"

"Who else could be here, my lord?" Salamatu asked in return, pretending to be surprised at such obviously unwarranted questions. "Danladi," Alhaji called.

"Rankadedel," Danladi answered as he came closer from the stance where he had positioned himself, watching the unfolding drama.

"What did you tell me?" Alhaji asked.

"I heard the voice of a man in this room. He was discussing with madam when I overheard his voice," Danladi affirmed.

"So where is the person?" Alhaji further asked.

"I suspect this one," Danladi said, pointing at Mustapha.

"Do you expect me to uncover a woman in ceremonial restriction?" Alhaji asked, not willing to violate the religious provisions he had always vehemently defended.

"I pledge my life that this person we see is not a woman. He is a man in disguise," Danladi insisted. "You are free to do whatever you wish to me if you find it contrary to my words."

"Woman, could we please confirm your identity?" Alhaji addressed Mustapha.

"Abomination, Alhaji! How could you desecrate the institution of marriage in this manner? This is somebody's wife; please," Salamatu protested.

Alhaji stood there, like one stuck in the mire. He was unable to move. It was a testing moment. He had to decide fast. Unveiling another man's wife was sacrilegious. He was convinced that if he unveiled her, and it turned out that she was a woman indeed, it could portend very grave consequences for him. His name would be rubbished. Within the provisions of the law, the husband of the disgraced woman could sue for libel and injury. The odds would favour that man to win such a case. He also could imagine what some men could do under extreme provocation. Some could take the law into their own hands and do the unthinkable.

However, Dauda knew that he could trust Danladi. Though he was just a driver, Danladi had long earned the trust of Alhaji Dauda. Most often, his reports about issues had always been credible and informed. He was not considered to be given to flippancy in any way. Whenever there were conflicting reports about any issue in the house, Danladi's voice had always been the deciding voice, provided he was present at the scene of the conflict-causing issue. Toeing the middle-of-the-road approach and letting the trouble-causing visitor go in peace could later create some other problems. Others would begin to see Danladi in the light of a rumour peddler and busybody. Danladi could as well choose to close his eyes and ears on everything he would witness in future, good or evil.

Juxtaposing these two possibilities created a real mental conflict within Alhaji. Finally, he seemed to regain his composure and sense of direction.

"Danladi!" he called. "Unveil him!" he said, taking a firm stand at last. Mustapha stood up. He did not resist Danladi's attempt to unveil him. Rather, he yielded himself, helping to make Danladi's assignment easier. Salamatu was scared. She just couldn't imagine what all that would lead to. Soon, the man was there for all to see. His mien was steely, indicating his readiness for whatever fate awaited him.

"Abominable sacrilege! *Ilia ila lai, Mohammadu Allah suru la!*" Alhaji muttered. Fondling his beads with his left hand, he turned to Salamatu.

"Why did you have the temerity to bring a man into my house, and right under my nose, eh?"

"And you," he said, pointing at Mustapha, "so you were not afraid to come into my house to defile my wife? Okay! Just hold on. I will show you what happens to criminals like you."

"With due respect, Alhaji, I have not committed any crime."

"Do you yet have the courage to talk?"

"Salamatu belongs to me. You only used the weapon of money to snatch her from me," Mustapha asserted, accusing Alhaji Dauda.

"What did you just say?" Alhaji asked.

"Yes, we were planning to marry before you and her parents suddenly decided otherwise."

"Salamatu, did you tell me you had a suitor?" Dauda asked Salamatu.

"My parents forbade me from speaking out," she confessed.

"Is the young man right, then? Do you still love him?" Salamatu could not immediately face up to answering that question.

"Do you still love him, Salamatu? Answer me now!"

"You have abandoned me, Alhaji," she said, sobbing. "Mustapha wouldn't abandon me."

"Okay then. Young man," he said, "would you be willing to take her as your wife now?"

I will, Alhaji."

"Very well, then. You both have twenty-four hours to leave my house. Go and pursue your happiness. I fault the tradition of giving out a girl in marriage without her expressly consenting to it. I shall vigorously channel my resources to ensure that some of these retrogressive customs are relaxed to meet the challenges of a fast-changing world."

CHAPTER 6.
PARTICULAR WAHALA

"Drambi! Drambi! *Tashi!*" Mariama called as she pushed and pulled Drambi, her husband. They have been married for thirteen years. She was concerned that Drambi might be late to work again today. Every day, he staggers back home very late in the night, with reddened eyes and offensive breath laced with the strong smell of alcohol. The image of Drambi looking like a lunatic always worried Mariama. Drambi's drinking habit was hardly ever suspended for one day. Deny him shots of locally brewed gin, and he'd be cross with everybody for the rest of the day. It was a chronic problem that needed a comprehensive package of solutions. As he lay on the bed that morning, snoring away his time, his children were almost ready for school. But their father Drambi had to be roused to give them money for bus fares to and from school.

Days without number, there had been several attempts by Mariama and the children to wake Drambi up when he was almost causing everybody to be late as a result of his inglorious drinking habit. Most often, however, such attempts always ended up causing more problems instead of providing answers. Today, as

Mariama tried to wake him up, she was apprehensive not to incur his wrath. At the same time, however, she was worried that her children might report late for school again. On days such as this, the children would always come back with reports of corporal punishment administered on them by the teachers. Mariama's grocery store had never opened early on days when Drambi was on morning duty. Drambi continuously caused such late opening which finally became the hallmark of the store.

"Drambi! The children are ready to go to school!" she pushed again.

"*Ah! Na shiga uku!*" he swore. "What kind of a cantankerous, nagging, stupid woman do I have for a wife?" he asked no one in particular as he lazily pulled his frame up and sat on the bed.

"Can't I enjoy some God-given rest for just a few minutes? Is it true that a man would go to work in the morning and come back late in the night, and all the welcome he gets is that everybody in the house keeps pestering him on a regular basis?"

"Good morning, Daddy!" little Jumai greeted him.

"Ah! Shut up! What's good about the morning when you and your mother never allow me to enjoy anything good about my life?" At that rebuke, the little girl shrank back, coldly withdrawing to the living room.

"Won't you go to work yourself?" Mariama asked.

"*Shh, shh!*" He ordered her to shut her mouth, placing his fore finger vertically over his lips.

"W-o-n-t you go to work?" he mimicked in mock fashion, baring his teeth and contorting his face. "When did you become my superior officer and timekeeper?"

"I apologize, my dear husband. The children need money for their transport to school."

"Eh-he! Money! Money! Money! The only thing I hear in this house is money, money and money."

"Dra-m-bi! Be reasonable for once! Why don't we stop this daily routine of heating up the house in the morning before going out for the day?"

"If you and your children would learn to stop truncating my morning rest, then everybody in the house would enjoy some peace. But if you continue troubling me; nobody will enjoy any form of rest."

"Okay, Drambi! We will talk about it later. Maybe you will learn to change your drinking habits."

"Ok! Am I the one to change, and not you? Drambi, stop drinking. Drambi, change your habits. Drambi this, Drambi that! Come, let me ask you: how many times have you seen me fight because of my so-called drinking habits?" he asked his wife.

"Okay, Drambi! We are not helping ourselves and the kids by engaging in this early-morning argument."

"What do we do then, Mrs Mariama Righteous?"

"Give them money for school. These kids are late!" she finally shouted, exasperated that Drambi was not forthcoming.

"Okay then," he said. "Since you have now become the commander-in-chief of Drambi Maigari's family, enforce your legislation by giving them money."

The children became tired of standing and watching as the situation deteriorated. They were resigned to their fate, sitting in the living room, not exactly certain if they would yet go to school that day or not. Jumai and her younger sister, Dinatu sat, hoping that the best would happen that morning. The school environment, despite all its inadequacies, was more comfortable for them than the home front. During the latter part of each day, their mother would unconsciously transfer all the aggression that should rightly be directed at their father towards them. As if the troubles from Drambi every night and morning were not enough, Mariama always added to them.

The school was different. The teachers were quite friendly. Jumai wondered if those teachers ever quarrelled in their homes. The smiling faces they wore every morning always made her believe they were free from all forms of trouble. Jumai envied them and their children. Her belief was strengthened by the lovely relationship that existed between teachers and pupils in that school. Though she was always whipped for late-coming, her class teacher drummed the belief into her that such beating was good for her. The teacher often said that she would not be doing her duty if she failed to discipline Jumai. A few times, she would bring up verses from the Christian holy book, the Bible, to support her action.

The teacher also probed severally to find out the root cause of Jumai's habitual lateness. But the poor little girl never opened up; she felt inwardly ashamed of the traditional quarrelling and fighting that went on between her parents every day. Her family's image in the neighbourhood was bad enough. On several occasions, other children who lived in the neighbourhood had used this to taunt Jumai and her younger siblings. Several times also, she had endured such taunts. But her humanity and developing pre-teenage psychology also prodded her on to the defence of her family. Often, whenever she adopted the defence option, she ended up fighting. Apparently, a revelation of the cause of her late-coming to the teacher might also cause trouble.

The peace and happiness Jumai and Dinatu enjoyed in school was worth so much to Jumai that she'd not barter them for anything. The beating, therefore, was the price she paid for happiness and peace. Therefore, she endured this also. Back home, her father literally terrorized every member of the family. She sometimes wished she were bigger than her father. She wished she were stronger and older. Then she'd give expression to her anger and frustration: then she'd sit him down and give him some tutorial on love and peace; then she'd force some of those bitter pills down his throat - those pills she herself had swallowed so many times. Yes! She'd tell him about her teacher in school, and how she makes everybody happy.

But Jumai was yet a twelve-year-old primary six pupil of Police Children School, Ikeja. Feminine and petite, she looked delicate and frail. Jumai was soft-spoken. She was developing into a beautiful Fulani girl with a steely, determined, defiant nature. She felt frustrated in her mind, almost mentally lost in the irony of a home that was more of a battlefield than a comfort zone. While this mental battle raged, she was oblivious to the physical brawl that had erupted between her parents. It was Dinatu who called Jumai's attention to the fight. That morning, it was obvious that the effect of the previous night's heavy liquor intake was yet to leave Drambi.

As Jumai stepped closer to the door linking the lounge and the bedroom, she stood at a safe distance and watched. Drambi and Mariama were engaged right in the bed. While they fought and struggled, standing and falling on the bed now and again, their two younger children, Ishaya and Dinatu were crying. Their focus alternated between Jumai and their parents as if Jumai had the power to stop the fight. Jumai continued to watch, betraying neither fear nor regret. The now permanently recurrent habit of cursing, quarrelling and fighting had become so common in that home that a day devoid of these was considered an extraordinary day.

The fight became more interesting to Jumai when she observed that the duellists were now on the floor of the room. Her mother had thrown her father down and sat atop him. Drambi's face was upwards. Mariama sat on his belly with one leg on either side of his torso. With both hands, she held him by the neck, her two knees holding down his arms while Drambi made frantic but fruitless efforts to be free. Obviously, he was beginning to choke. He was too weak to fight like a man. Mariama, while maintaining her vantage position, extracted a promise from Drambi to the effect that he'd provide the money when released from her grip. Thereafter, she stood up, releasing Drambi.

The children did go to school that day, but not before Drambi had drunk full of the cup of shame. Before the fight ended, the noise of the combatants and that of the crying children attracted neighbours to the scene. The neighbourhood was a low-income housing estate built by the government of the Federal Republic for men of the Police Force. Over the years, the estate had suffered neglect of inexplicable magnitude. The central sewage disposal system had long ceased to function effectively. Most septic pipes, not well buried, had surfaced as a result of heavy rains over successive seasons. Some were already broken due to long exposure to extreme weather and careless human activities. As the waste found its way to the cesspool, those open spots served as outlets for decomposing organic waste. Some waste settled in accumulations at convenient spots. Others formed tributaries feeding the larger settlements.

Domestic chickens, ducks, and turkeys waded through these semi-liquid masses in search of their daily bread. Human activity also progressed in so regular a manner that a first-time visitor would wonder if the inhabitants have any iota of sanity remaining in them. Eating and drinking joints were scattered all over the estate. Various kinds of music continuously played in conflicting and confusing tradition, creating some difficulties for ears to discern the tunes being played. The noise from these forced persons within the neighbourhood to speak in unusually high tones. As far as the inhabitants were concerned, life was sweet and must be lived to the full.

Since the properties belonged to the Federal Government, occupants displayed zero-level obligations on the issues of maintenance and/or effecting repairs on some of the dilapidated structures. On their part, those in government were too pre-occupied with "matters of governance" to pay attention to an old low-income housing estate in such state of disrepair. It is the business of governments here to award contracts, build and allocate structures. It is hardly the interest of governments in this part of the world to maintain such structures.

In this estate, water was scarce. This does not translate to unavailability of water. It only means that potable water was not within reach. The water scheme serving the estate had also gone the way of other amenities. The tanks were dried up. Initially, residents resorted to buying water from commercial water tankers and vendors. The coming of the rains was always very good news for this neighbourhood. Rainwater was all-purpose water. Though all the houses were roofed with asbestos sheets, nobody cared about the health implications of drinking this water. The cost of buying water was high. The fact that every family could save about that much was a welcome development. Such money was enough to buy corn pap for the entire family daily. In Drambi Maigari's home, for instance, pap and bean cake, popularly called *akara*, was the preferred breakfast staple.

This morning, Drambi reluctantly provided the money requested by the children. He was particularly angry that part of the money he had reserved for local gin was gone. "Misappropriation!" he said to himself. He comforted himself with the resolve that the burden of paying for his drinks must be indirectly borne by somebody yet unknown. And the ones who easily came to mind were drivers of commercial buses that plied the route where he'd be on stop and search duty that morning. He set out, quite disguised. Looking at him, there was nothing to suggest he was a cop. His shoes would not be too easy for the common man to distinguish. His uniform trousers and shirt were-neatly folded and tucked into a cellophane carrier bag. His beret was equally folded and carefully concealed in his trouser pocket. This way, his identity as a policeman was effectively hidden.

This is done for the principal purpose of avoiding or at least reducing the possibilities of attack by men of the underworld. In this country, armed robbers see military and para-military personnel as enemies. One feature that is common to these groups is the uniform dress-code. Often, when armed robbers waylay a bus and attack, uniformed men are always prime targets for elimination. They are considered a security risk by hoodlums. Based on this, there evolved this unwritten code, faithfully adhered to by officers and men of the police, to dress up in mufti while on their way to or from work.

Drambi stood at the bus stop, waiting to catch a bus. The fog on his mind was yet to totally clear. He knew he had challenges to meet, but his mind was not completely clear enough to chart a course of action. The month was yet to end. Another salary might take two or more weeks to come. Though he rakes in money, almost daily, he wondered where all the money goes. For several years now he had not visited his village. The few times he had run into one or two members of his extended family or old friends, he'd always felt like burying his face in shame. He was never prepared. Never prepared to meet them! At first, he'd try to pretend he did not see them. But they were always excited to call his name and exchange pleasantries. Then they'd probe to know more about his well-being, about where he stayed; about everything.

Well, he always invented a story. Sometimes he lied to them that he was serving in Ikot-Nakanda, Cross River State. He knew they may not be too keen on visiting. When they probed further, he'd be quick to add that he was always on special duties that most often took him out of the state; or that he was attending one course or the other. He regretted that he always had to lie. He had a complex - the complex that he ought to be more advanced in life; more advanced than the base life of squalor to which he sentenced himself and his family.

Now, as always, there was no money to run the home. Recurrently, Mariama would make a thousand and one demands. If it is not that the pot of soup made two days earlier was exhausted, it would be that kerosene was totally dried up in the stove. Garri, pepper, soap, rice, beans, yam, bread, sachets of milk, crayfish, seasonings, water, and bus fares, ah! So many things! And school fees are paid at the beginning of every term. Garments for the kids, school uniforms, books, and electricity bills! *"Akwoi wahala so sei!"* he exclaimed in soliloquy.

Drambi's problem was multi-faceted. He knew this very well. He considered himself lucky enough to be favoured by his superior officers in that he was always included in the number of officers and men going for routine "stop and search" duty on busy roads. While on such duty, the practice has been to extort money from commercial road users and a few private motorists who might be unlucky enough to contravene traffic laws. And he had done well. He has done well because, besides the monetary target always set for his group to meet, he had always gone back to the Officer in Charge (O.C.) to duly register his appreciation. This habit endeared him to his superior officers. He was the envy of some other men of the rank and file. Yet, he had nothing to show for it.

In the service, every day was a working day. But the average cop worked for eight hours a day; they also worked on shifts. Drambi's day was always full. After a successful day of extortions, he would join his colleagues to go to the office, make returns to the big man, and share their own portion of the money. When this was done, he'd change into his mufti again and hit the road.

On such days, his first port of call would be Ngozi's apartment in Mafoluku, Oshodi. Ngozi was a fair-skinned young woman of Igbo extraction. She was a petty trader at the popular Oshodi market. During a joint raid of the market by soldiers and policemen, Drambi met Ngozi. She was one of the traders arrested for obstructing Oshodi railway with their wares. He took a liking to Ngozi immediately, so he pleaded with his colleagues that Ngozi was his girlfriend. He facilitated Ngozi's release. Later, he followed up on Ngozi, and a relationship was born. Neither Ngozi nor Drambi envisaged the kind of bond that would later develop.

Drambi spent more money on Ngozi and drinks than he spent on his family. He rented and furnished Ngozi's apartment. He rented a new lock-up shop for her. By a silent agreement, Drambi also became the breadwinner here. When Ngozi complained of requiring a helping hand at home and suggested bringing one of her younger siblings to Lagos, Drambi felt no qualms about that. When the lad came, Drambi picked up the bills for his upkeep and education. Drambi's daily routine on such days of financial buoyancy was monotonous. Ngozi's house was the place for relaxation. Drambi spent most of his happy moments there. Whenever he had one social function or the other to attend, he always did so in the company of Ngozi.

Drambi was a generous man whenever he was with Ngozi, and a miser whenever he was with his family. He often mentally compared his wife with Ngozi. His wife was a good woman; there was no doubt about that. But she always nagged. She always accused him of excessive drinking. She was always ready to bandy words with him. They also exchanged blows regularly. She was already a mother of four kids and had lost some of those youthful feminine features that attracted a man.

Mariama did not care so much about her outward appearance. While at home, she was fond of wrapping the lower part of her body with a piece of cloth, in typical African fashion; and the upper frame she covered with just anything called a blouse. She never applied make-up. There were times that her hair would emit some poignant odour. At other times, her hair was either covered with a scarf or plaited in some Afrooriented style. Most times, she considered it worrisome when reminded that she should take a bath in the evening before going to bed.

Yet, Mariama was simply a good woman. She was kind-hearted and affectionate. She took good care of the kids. Mariama was the launderer at home. She ensured that everybody's garments were always clean. She ironed them also. She never failed in entertaining visitors. She always prayed and taught the children to pray. Strangely enough, she seldom attended church services, but always ensured that the children went to church every Sunday. Above all, she was a comparatively good manager of money.

On the other hand, Ngozi was more of a spendthrift. She was a believer in the theory that for money to come, one must spend money. She often stated that money develops wings and flies away from the man who does not spend it. It was her confessed opinion that if money is not spent, it loses the very essence of its existence. Ngozi was a church girl. She never missed her Sunday services. And she could tell about almost all the mega-churches in town. She visited any church of her choice on any given day. Yet, she was careful enough not to be counted as a very committed member of any of those churches. She detested any proposal by members of any church to visit. She often gave them wrong addresses whenever she filled their forms.

At home, she'd pray first thing in the morning and last thing at night before going to bed. She knew how to carry problems to God in prayers. She believed that God is a God of love and is ever-ready to forgive sins. Ngozi's temperament could rise to boiling point when she was annoyed. She believed in herself. She would always look herself in the mirror and call out admiringly, "Ngo baby!" It was her conviction that she must take good care of herself before any other consideration. She was very careful about her appearance- careful to the minutest details.

Her make-up kit was always full. Her powder range was complete with foundation, pressed and loose powder. Then lipsticks and lip-liners; eye pencils and enhancers; mascaras; hand and face cream; lotions, night cream and assorted hair cream and conditioners; nail varnish; antiperspirant spray, designer fragrance and deodorant; hair kits and treatment materials. Every week, Ngozi wore a new hairstyle. For every social engagement she'd attend, whether in the company of Drambi or with some other person, Ngozi made it a point of duty to either make or buy a new garment. She always wore sweet-smelling perfume.

Youthful and well endowed, Ngozi was sedulous in her resolve to ensure that Drambi's heart was permanently and repeatedly stolen by her seductive looks. Poor Drambi! He was too weak to resist such temptation. Ngozi never argued with Drambi, yet she always got more than she asked for. She often bought him beer, yet mildly advised him to be moderate with alcohol. She expressed gratitude for everything she received from him, yet she never failed to utilize every opportunity to assert that it takes a lot of money to make a woman look good and attractive.

Those were things Drambi considered as he stood at the bus stop that morning, sunk in the misery that surrounded his person. He wondered what to do with his life. Ngozi was obviously doing well. "What about his family?" he thought. His wife and children were living from hand to mouth. He was like a man living under a spell. But Ngozi seemed to always make him happy. He was always happy in her company. Whichever way, there was something about Ngozi that brought happiness to him. As he reasoned along this line, shouts of "Osho-di-o! Osho-di-o!! Osho-di-o!!!" suddenly made him come to himself. Looking up, he saw a big locally fabricated bus, otherwise known as a *"molue"*, about to pull up for intending commuters to board.

He positioned himself to join others in the struggle to board. Incidentally, he failed. Afterwards, he was able to secure a space in a smaller Mitsubishi L-300 fourteen-seater bus. When the bus conductor began to collect the fares, Drambi adjusted his position, reaching into his right pocket with his hand, as though he was ensuring that his cap was in place. As soon as the conductor asked him to pay, Drambi pulled out his beret and uttered "staff".

The word "staff" is a general word used to indicate that the claimant is a man or officer of any of the military or Para-military services. As a fallout of repeated intimidation, coercion, and abuse of office, these uniformed men successfully excluded themselves from paying intra-city bus fares in major cities in Nigeria. A driver or conductor who insisted on them paying their bus fares would only be exposing himself to grave consequences and unimaginable future danger. Such a driver would instantly get blacklisted and be dealt with severely and with little or no provocation. Funny enough, there's no legislation in this country that warranted such acts as these. Ironically, this is so brazenly done that even the occupier of the nation's number-one political seat of power could not feign ignorance of it.

Military personnel here had become a law unto themselves. Not only that, but they had equally compelled the civil populace to perceive the military from the military's point of view: above the law. And this country's civil society, either by reason of ingrained cowardice, or deep-rooted penchant for self-preservation, or a combination of both factors, had willingly surrendered some of their basic rights to the men and women of the force. It was, therefore, normal under the circumstance for Drambi to announce to the bus conductor that he was staff. Interestingly, these policemen were not totally inconsiderate. They managed to retain some degree of fairness and rationality, even if those were remnants of the integrity that these men and women possessed before joining the service. The benefits of being staff on a commercial bus in the city of Lagos were not exclusively advantageous to these uniformed men. Commercial bus drivers also reaped from that lopsided equation contrived as a balm to soothe this permanently festering wound.

A commercial bus driver saves himself some money when he has "staff" on board by announcing so whenever he encounters a roadblock mounted by the police. Such a driver is excluded from having his vehicle "particulars" checked. He, therefore, does not pay the mandatory fifty naira or any other money the policemen in their wisdom might demand. It is imperative to note that whereas relevant authorities had permanently fixed amounts as fines for various traffic offences, the police indiscriminately imposed any amount on motorists, depending on several factors.

The clear-minded disposition of the policeman engaging a motorist at a given time would go a long way to determine how humane or beastly the policeman would be at that time. The financial state of the team's collective purse at the time of intercepting a vehicle also mattered. If the team was yet to rake in a large enough sum of money, their attitude towards motorists could only be likened to that of a hungry lion when he is face to face with a sheep without a shepherd. But if their hearts were already joyous due to a bagful of squeezed naira notes, such joy always found a way of expressing itself on the face of the cop. At times like this, their zeal may wane considerably.

As soon as Drambi got to his station at Ikeja, he immediately changed into his official uniform and reported to the office of his boss, the Divisional Police Officer. The D.P.O., Mr Nkereuwem Ekpo, was a Chief Superintendent of Police. An Efik, he hailed from Nko in Obubra Local Government Area of Cross River state, South-South Nigeria. Mr Ekpo was a man of average height whose stomach was rather too big and quite disproportionate to his height. If Ekpo were to be a woman, his protruding stomach might house a twenty-four-week-old foetus.

"Morning, sir!" Drambi saluted.

"Good morning, Sergeant Drambi", Ekpo responded. "How are you?"

"Fine, sir!"

"Why are you always late to work whenever you are on morning duty?"

"My wife took ill in the night, sir! I had to take her to the clinic this morning, sir!"

"Does your wife take ill every day?"

"No, sir! Just today, sir!"

"Why then do you always report late?"

"I'll change, sir! I promise, sir! I am sorry, sir!"

"You know I always want you to be in the team going for stop and search."

"Yes, sir!"

"It's not because we lack men. It's simply because you always tell me the truth, and I need a man I can trust at all times."

"Yes, sir! I will always be true, sir!"

"So, how is your wife currently?"

"She's responding to treatment, sir!"

"Other members of the team are waiting for you. Go and join them."

"Yes, sir!"

"As long as you remain sincere, I will ensure you do not lack money, unless I am posted out of this station. Goodbye!"

"Bye, sir!"

Drambi walked briskly to a waiting Toyota Hilux Pick-up van where other members of the team had assembled. As soon as Drambi arrived, they all jumped into the vehicle. The team leader, an Inspector of Police, sat in the front with the driver, a sergeant. Other members of the team, numbering eight, settled in the rear compartment. Some of these sat on the semi-permanent seats facing either side of the road. The rest sat on the tailboard, holding parts of the roof structure for support.

The illegally acquired authority of these cops also included, but was not limited to, contravening traffic laws when nothing was at stake. It was not surprising, then, to see the police team drive against the normal flow of traffic, temporarily converting that side of the road meant for vehicular movement to Ikeja and Mangoro. They had their headlights on full beam. The siren fitted to the vehicle also blared, as a warning to vehicles coming from the opposite direction to give way. Completing the cycle of irrationality were two members of the team who stood on either side of the tailboard, holding horse-whips, ready to assault any road user who, by omission or commission, failed to heed the message being jointly passed across by the beaming headlights and siren.

Despite driving against the traffic, they engaged in such breath-taking speed that other road users were bewildered. In their astonishment, some of those road users pulled up on the side of the road or reduced their own speed to allow the cops free access. This practice by the police team is equally common among political office holders, police chiefs and military top brass. In this country, all men are not considered equal. Participation in Government or appointment into a high office meant being elevated above certain laws of the land. The higher the position, the more qualified the holder of that office is to defy as many laws as he chooses to.

"Oga!" Drambi called. "*We no go branch for bunker?*"

"We are going there *oh jare!*" the team leader replied.

"Sergeant!" The inspector addressed the driver. "We'll get to the bunker before anything else."

"All correct, sir!" the driver affirmed.

They drove through Adekunle Fajuyi Way and parked beside a complex fully installed with communications equipment owned by the Federal Radio Corporation. Sharing a common boundary with this outfit was the Oshodi end of Ikeja Military Cantonment. Between Agege motor road and Ikeja G.R.A. are a rail-line and some stretches of bush on either side of the railway. Along one stretch, some artisans and petty traders erected temporary sheds, selling goods and services. A shed was far removed from others. This was the bunker.

As the vehicle stopped by the roadside, Drambi and some of his colleagues walked to the shack at the extreme and helped themselves to wraps of marijuana. The team leader and two others bought locally brewed gin from a nearby shed. They all ate in a makeshift cafeteria there. Soon, they were done.

"Thank you, oga!" Constable Wunmi said.

"Never mind! I hope everybody can work now?"

"Yes, sir!" they answered.

"My mind is very clear now, oga," Drambi said.

The Inspector ignored him.

In no time, the team arrived at P.W.D. bus stop, which was a few hundred meters away from the bunker. They decided to work there for the day. After receiving their brief, three of the men were sent across Agege motor road to intercept vehicles going towards Oshodi from Ikeja, Sango-Otta, Cement, Egbeda, Akowonjo, Iyana-Ipaja, Idimu, Dopemu, Agege, and some other areas. This group operated from the Shogunle side of the road. Three other cops, including Drambi, were stationed to stop and search vehicles coming out of Oshodi to any of the places outlined above. The other three manned the road that led into Ikeja G.R.A. They were responsible for dealing with vehicles coming from Lagos Island, Ketu, Maryland, Yaba, and some other suburbs.

Their leader, the Inspector, sat in the vehicle, monitoring the exercise. It was business as usual for the police team. They ordered every commercial vehicle to stop. Some private vehicles were not spared either. As commercial buses approached from any of the triangular routes, some policemen held their rifles, assuming the postures of battle-ready soldiers. Such postures were enough to send the right signal to road users that the business of the day was very serious indeed. Others engaged in collecting the compulsory 'toll fees' from drivers. While extorting money from drivers, the policemen issued numbers to every vehicle.

It was now the new norm to issue serial numbers to all vehicles whose drivers had paid the mandatory fifty naira imposed on them. The numbering system was the outcome of deep research of the rank and file's think-tank over some smart drivers' spurious claims that they had paid such money on earlier trips. The police, therefore, devised that as a means of reducing and eliminating cases of such claims by those "fraudulent drivers". All the same, it was a rat-race in this country. To date, the police and commercial bus drivers continue to invent new methods of out-manoeuvring each other.

When drivers discovered that policemen were getting smarter every day, they also dug deep into their minds, excavating and putting into useful activity the rich deposits of human intelligence in them. It did not matter if this intelligence was negative or not. In this country, it is believed that man must fully utilize all the survival instincts in him. Otherwise, he might not survive in a world like ours.

On a given day, a police team might decide to issue numbers 91- 100. If a driver approached and announced his number, he would be easily identified. Drivers also knew they were playing a risky game. If a driver was caught lying with the intent to evade payment of fifty naira, he was forced to pay a higher, outrageous amount. Defaulting drivers could also have their ignition keys confiscated, and they would be delayed indefinitely. The police had no regard whatsoever for commuters who were usually affected by such decisions to delay the bus.

Since most Lagosians had learnt by experience that it was tantamount to committing suicide for a passenger to confront the police on this, their frustrations were always directed at the drivers. Passengers aboard those commercial buses always blamed drivers who tried to evade payment of those imposed fees. By so doing, they lent credence to the legality of those fees. Some commuters went further to justify the practice, opining they were practical examples of the law of sowing and reaping- that drivers charged indiscriminate fares without consideration for the impoverished and pauperized man on the street.

Such positions were not borne out of nowhere. Drivers always exploited commuters. Opportunities for such exploitation presented themselves regularly. One of such recurring opportunities was the new institutionalized government-regulated upward adjustment of prices of petroleum products. Besides the regimented pricing of these products, the monster of fuel scarcity had long been a regular symbol of economic pain, virtually affecting everybody in any part of this country. The argument against operators in the transport sector, therefore, was not that prices of petroleum products were not increased now and again, but that those operators used such adjustments as excuses to hike transportation fares to ridiculously outrageous levels.

Several times, that had resulted in civil unrest across the country. On this basis, therefore, commuters hardly empathized with drivers whenever the latter were being forced to part with some money. On the contrary, most commuters saw that as a good opportunity to have their pound of flesh from drivers, even though those commuters had no iota of love for the policemen either.

As Drambi and his colleagues continued in their business of extortion, they barked out orders to drivers asking them to *"roja"*—a euphemism for 'settlement' and cooperation. On this outing, Inspector

Ibe and his team issued unique identification numbers to commercial vehicles. The names of five communities in the Ibibio/Efik-speaking area of South-southern Nigeria were being issued as numbers. Drivers were surprised to receive numbers like "Ikot-abasi; Ikot-ansa; Ikot-ekpene; Ikot-osurua; and Uyo. That was in furtherance of the search for the elusive solution to false claims being made by some drivers.

At about two o'clock that afternoon, Inspector Ibe called the attention of a teenager hawking sausage rolls.

"Hey, gala! Come!" he shouted. The girl turned and looked in the direction of Ibe, expecting a confirmation.

"You no dey hear?" Ibe reiterated the invitation. The poor girl enthusiastically walked towards Ibe, expecting to sell.

"Take this money and buy ten bottles of soft drinks over there for us," he said, pointing across the expressway. Before the girl could take five steps, Ibe re-called her.

"Drop your gala for that vehicle," Ibe commanded, asking the girl to place the box of sausage rolls in the vehicle, pointing to the rear of the police van.

"But make sure say you count am o! I no want wahala", he said, advising the girl to take a record of the pieces of sausage rolls she was leaving behind.

Within him, he was afraid that the girl could abscond with the money. Asking her to keep those sausage rolls was more of safeguarding his interest than lightening the girl's burden. Ironically, it was good news for the girl when she returned. Those policemen bought twenty pieces of Gala sausage rolls from her. To sell so many pieces at once was delightful. Every member of the team took his turn to come and refresh himself. Drambi was yet to come over when an argument ensued between him and the driver of a locally fabricated bus.

"Clear well! Clear very well!" Drambi said, commanding the driver to pull up by the roadside.

"Oga sergeant, I just dey comot now" the driver said, trying to excuse himself on the basis that he had just resumed work for the day.

"I say clear! Abi you no dey hear?" Drambi shouted angrily.

"Oga, na from mechanic shop we just de comot now. We never make one trip," the driver appealed, informing that he'd been at the mechanic shop almost all day fixing his bus.

"Give me your particulars and clear very well," Drambi insisted, issuing the final warning.

"Okay, sir," the driver finally said, pretending to comply. He had earlier pleaded with the police corporal collecting money from motorists on that side of the road. Drambi, who had earlier been in a combat-ready position with his rifle in his hand, had intervened to compel the bus driver to pay. When he saw that the driver was adamantly bent on not parting with a single dime, Drambi ordered the driver to move to a spot and turn off his engine. However, the driver tried to pull a fast one on the cops.

He engaged gear in an apparent bid to speed off. Unfortunately, he could neither escape Drambi's watchful eyes nor ready hands. Drambi pointed the barrel of his rifle towards the bus and simultaneously pulled the trigger. There was a bang. Shouts and cries filled the air. Pandemonium broke out. Everybody tried to scamper to safety. Meanwhile, a shrill cry of *"ekpa mi o! ekpa mi o!"* was heard on the bus. The bus finally pulled up a few meters away from that spot. The bullet from Drambi's rifle had hit a pregnant woman in the head. She was bleeding and managed to scream with the last ounce of strength in her. As the bus stopped, some passengers tried to nurse the woman. However, she was determined to follow the path of her departed forebears and gave up the ghost.

Some other passengers quickly alighted and took to their heels. The brave ones among them immediately started a song and charged towards the policemen. In solidarity, some other motorists and social miscreants joined in the march. The blood-soaked body of the slain woman, obviously in the last trimester of pregnancy, was carried shoulder-high by some of the men as they sang along:

How - many - people - olokpa - go - kill?
How - many - people - olokpa - go - kill?
Eh - dem - go - kill - us - tire
Eh - dem - go - kill - us - tire
Eh - eh - eh - dem - go - kill - us - tire
How - many - people - olokpa - go - kill?

The policemen, sensing danger and obviously lacking the requisite wisdom for crisis management, fired into the air to scare and possibly disperse the ever-increasing crowd. That act worsened an already volatile situation. The protesting crowd now seemed more determined to accomplish their mission. The cops, getting more confused as the commotion increased, ran towards the patrol vehicle. But they were not as lucky as they'd wish. Before they could all mount, the rioters had quickly surrounded the vehicle.

They were now irrevocably committed to making a statement with some vengeful acts. Some young men, not exactly aware of the genesis of the riots, joined the fray. They were enjoying the hysteria of such wild, free-for-all, uncontrolled, and unhindered access to express some violent emotion. The crowd pounced on the police vehicle. The cops, as if by some magical prowess, or sheer cleverness and ability to wriggle out of difficulty, had all abandoned the vehicle, having pulled off their shirts and berets. Some stripped themselves down to their underwear, in a frantic effort to escape identification.

But then, the crowd already knew some of those tricks. In the ensuing scuffle, three policemen were hacked to death. The patrol vehicle was set ablaze, but not before it had been completely vandalized. Some of the young men struggled for the contents of the Cellophane bag that served as the central purse of the police team. Five members of the team escaped unhurt. This included Drambi. Inspector Ibe and Constable Wunmi were not that lucky. Both were seriously injured by the rampageous crowd.

The song of the crowd thereafter turned into that of victory.

Taking over the roads, they marched forth and back chanting:

Nzogbu! Enyimba enyi!
Nzogbu! Enyimba enyi!
Nzogbu nzogbu!
Enyimba enyi!

The mob resorted to searching every vehicle that dared to drive along any of those roads. Most motorists, informed on the riots, decided to take alternative routes to their destinations. Some miscreants among the mob also looted shops within Shogunle-Ladipo axis. Drambi was lucky enough to have found refuge in a building on Isaac John Street, G.R.A., Ikeja.

While running for his dear life, he had seen the gate leading into this house opening, and a car driving out. He wasted no time in utilizing that opportunity to save himself. He ran into the compound without permission. The gatekeeper was puzzled and stared at Drambi. Drambi continued running into the main building and looking back to see if the rioters were coming after him. The gatekeeper, being confused himself, forgot to lock up the gate. He chased after Drambi, shouting "hei! hei! Where are you going?"

Drambi did not utter a word. He motioned with his hands, appealing to the man to lock the gate. The gateman quickly ran to the gate and locked it up. Thereafter, he went back to Drambi. Drambi, in his singlet, trousers and shoes neither looked like a mentally sick person nor a rational thinking nor balanced person. The gateman knew something must be wrong with this man who had forced his way into the compound. He became apprehensive while approaching Drambi.

"Yes oga! Wetin happen?" he asked.

"I am a policeman," Drambi answered.

The gateman re-assessed Drambi. Looking at Drambi from head to toe, he seemed to be prying to confirm the truth or otherwise of Drambi's claims. His eyes probed Drambi's body. Then he noticed Drambi's trousers. They looked like a policeman's trousers. However, that was not enough to convince him. It was strange to him. He had never anticipated seeing a policeman on the road looking like that.

"Are you a policeman for real?"

"Yes, sir!"

"Then why are you looking like a madman?" he asked further.

"Trouble! There's trouble! They almost killed me over there,"

Drambi answered.

"Oh!" the man exclaimed, trying to link Drambi with the riot which he just got a hint of through the driver who brought his master's children back from school. That was the same driver who was driving out when Drambi ran into the house.

"Are you coming from that riot at P.W.D.?"

"Yes! They almost killed us there!"

"Ah! But you policemen wicked oh! I hear say una don kill many civilians for that place."

"It's not true! It's not true! Hide me, please."

"Walahi talahi!" the gateman swore.

"If not for Allah, I would have killed you myself. Follow me!" he commanded Drambi as he led Drambi to the rear of the house. He opened a room in the boys' quarters and ushered Drambi in.

"You no go fit stay here for too long so my oga no go see you oh," the gateman warned. "Another thing be say I go lock this door carry the key comot," he added, indicating he would temporarily lock Drambi up for the security of both of them and the property.

"I'll do this because I don't really know you. You know this is Lagos where everything is possible. My duty post is actually at the gate," he added.

He locked Drambi up in the room, taking the keys with him. Drambi breathed a sigh of relief. He felt safe to some degree. Now, his mind could work again. He reached for his mobile phone. He was not very certain he still had it. Searching his pockets, he found it. His agony and fright were temporarily relieved by the optimism that he'd soon communicate with his boss, the Divisional Police Officer, Mr Nkereuwem Ekpo. He dialled Ekpo's number. No success! He dialled again…and again. Then came that programmed familiar voice with the message:

'The number you have dialled is not available at the moment. Please try again later'.

"No! Not at this time," Drambi soliloquized. More efforts to connect with Ekpo created more frustration. Then a message appeared on the screen of his handset: NETWORK PROBLEM.

He was disappointed that at such a crucial time as this, the network was failing. He gave some thought to this: the network always seemed to have a way of disappointing at very important periods. He was still trying to think up a solution when the gateman opened the door and announced to him that his time was up.

"Oga police, you have to leave now. My master will come back anytime now."

Meanwhile, the crowd of protesters at P.W.D. had thinned down considerably because they observed that their common enemies had either been lynched or escaped the scene. However, some of them continued in the rampage, mounting roadblocks and extorting money from innocent motorists. Others clustered in groups, not only discussing the shooting of the pregnant woman by the police, but also the attendant visitation of wrath upon the police team. The lifeless bodies of the slain policemen were mangled beyond recognition. Each head was beaten to a pulp, forcing the brains to come out in a mass. Blood and abdominal fluids, which earlier spurted out of the bodies as a result of desecration, were scattered all over the tarred roads.

The scoundrels continued to hold sway until one of them raised an alarm that the police were coming. Three lorryloads of fierce-looking mobile policemen arrived on the scene, apparently declaring war on the protesters. They shot without recourse to caution, sending shockwaves down the spines of many, announcing their presence and their readiness to engage any group. No sooner had the police trucks stopped and the policemen began to jump out than the young men and women took to their heels. They all disappeared into neighbouring slums.

With disappointed looks on their faces, made so because of their inability to wreak havoc among the protesters and avenge their colleagues, those policemen also transferred their aggression to motorists. Motorists driving along Agege motor road were compelled to stop, turn off their engines and alight. They were thoroughly searched and extensively interrogated. A good number of them had their heads hit with the butt of a rifle. Some others received very hot slaps in the face for daring to ask questions. Yet others were subjected to some other forms of assault, including being asked to strip to their underwear, and then roll on the hot tarred road.

Next, they visited their wrath on the bus whose driver's argument with Drambi had been the genesis of the brouhaha. The policemen simply siphoned petrol from the tank of a car and sprinkled this on the engine compartment and seats of the bus. They ignited a matchstick and threw it into the bus. They felt highly relieved when they saw the fierce and violent rage of the fire serving their purpose. At least some degree of vengeance has been achieved. Sporadically, they shot into the air, warning the neighbourhood that their mission was yet to be accomplished.

It was not until dusk that they carried the mangled bodies of their slain colleagues into one of the trucks and left the vicinity for their station. During the evening news broadcast of a popular private television station, more inhabitants of the city of Lagos and beyond got to know details of the cause and results of the violent disorder. In the report, the newscaster announced that four lives were lost as a result of an argument between a policeman on a roadblock and a commercial bus driver over the payment of fifty naira illegally demanded by the policemen. Citing an eyewitness account, the station invited one Mrs Iyabo Olumuyiwa, whose sobriquet was "Iya Amebo", to shed more light on the issue. "*Na true sha,*" Iya Amebo began. "*Na paticula wahala.*"

"What do you mean by particular wahala?" the reporter asked.

"It's as a result of the stop and search duty police officers at P.W.D. They were extorting money from commercial drivers. When they stopped this particular vehicle, the driver pleaded with one of them that he had been at the mechanic shop all day long, and hadn't made any trip earlier. Based on that, the policeman asked him to pull up by the roadside and tender his driving and vehicle licence, or his particulars as they normally call these.

"The driver duly complied, handing over every document requested to him. This infuriated the policeman. He accused the driver of playing a huge joke. He asked the driver if those documents could buy him anything, and further insisted that the vehicle must properly pull up.

"The driver deciphered the handwriting on the wall: that the policemen were really not interested in those documents but in money. He became angry. The driver seemed frustrated by the policeman's total lack of empathy. He tried to pull a fast one, attempting to drive off. As soon as the vehicle wheels rolled, I heard the deafening sound of gunshot, and an accompanying shrill cry beside me. As I looked, I was jolted to see that the bullet not only pierced the head of a pregnant woman sitting next to me, but that she was instantly killed. Is that not particulars-related trouble? *Abi no be particula wahala?*"

"Thank you, Iya Amebo. Greg Williams reporting."

The following morning, the police authorities issued a statement rejecting what they called the "biased, unconfirmed, prejudiced and inciting report" of the television station. The police claimed that the reports reaching them confirmed that the bus was carrying members of an ethnic militia, notorious for their antigovernment stance. Furthermore, they continued, unconfirmed reports had it that the militiamen had planned, and were on their way to execute an ethnic cleansing agenda when they ran out of luck and encountered the police who were on routine stop and search duty. The policemen, unaware of what the mission of those people was, were only trying to ask normal questions when the militia men opened fire on the police team. Unfortunately, during an exchange of gunfire, a stray bullet hit a pregnant woman.

The police authorities, however, admitted that investigations had not been concluded, adding that as soon as they were, the outcome would be made public. They promised to deal extensively with, and summarily dismiss from service, any policeman found wanting through the reports of the Special Investigative Panel. They also urged the public to remain calm and co-operate with the police in the fight against crime. Lastly, they affirmed their readiness to protect the civil populace, reminding the public that the police are their friends.

It's been years already. Characteristic of investigations, probes, and enquiries in this country, no mention has been made of this issue. The police, even today, freely extort money from road users. This is done in the full glare of the public. Sadly enough, each new government pretends not to know what goes on.

The apathy of government is understood since most government functionaries cannot claim to be clean themselves. The ordinary Nigerian citizen remains a harassed and bewildered man who is being dehumanized, not only by social miscreants and hoodlums but also by the government and various agencies created to enforce the law.

CHAPTER 7.
FLYING COLOURS

Justice Innocent Ezedinaobi (retd) was happy. It was one of those moments when a man felt satisfied and fulfilled. He was happy with Afamefuna, his son. His joy stemmed from the news that Afamefuna had distinguished himself at the last University Matriculation Examinations, organized by the Joint Admissions Bureau. Young Afam had scored three hundred and eighty-six points. That was a record-breaking mark. For the past fifteen years, nobody had achieved that feat in Nigeria. It was, therefore, a feat worthy of acclaim. Ezedinaobi and his family heard the pleasantly surprising news on the radio. Besides announcing this, the examination body had equally offered to include the name of this brilliant and high-scoring student in the bureau's hall of fame.

Twenty-four hours after the breaking of that wonderful news, both the Federal and Imo state governments, at separate forums, announced full scholarship for the celebrated lad. Throughout that week, the home of the Ezedinaobis was a beehive. Visitors kept trooping in to congratulate the youth who had brought glory to his family and village. Based on this, Ezedinaobi and his family had requested that the Catholic diocese of Oguta hold a special thanksgiving service. At the service, the Reverend ·S. O. Mmereole, the diocesan father, used the opportunity to encourage other youths to work hard, reminding them that such feats could only be possible when a student diligently pursues his studies.

"Are you not surprised?" Ogonna asked Ngwoni in whispers, despite the ongoing holy mass. "How did water find its way into the gourd?"

"Why do you ask such questions?" Ngwoni asked in response. "We are in church," he reminded Ogonna.

"Don't assume your 'holier than thou' posture," Ogonna warned.

"Is it not written that the Sabbath was made for man, and that man was not made for the Sabbath? Reverend Father Ngwoni! Everybody knows that Afam is a blockhead. Moreover, he never ever made time to study. So, how did he suddenly become so brilliant as to be the number one in Nigeria?"

"Have you never heard that examinations are not the true test of knowledge? Besides, our University Matriculation Examinations are designed as objective questions with options. Luck could just be on the side of any fool."

They were both in the same school as Afamefuna.

"There is definitely no such thing as luck in examinations. You either know the answers or you don't," Ogonna stated with emphasis.

"So why are you surprised at Afam's stunning success?"

"I am surprised because he is my classmate! I know he is the least-qualified student to top a class in examinations, much less to talk of leading the whole nation."

"In that case, what will you do about it?"

"Nothing! It's only that I strongly smell a rat in all this. My father's most popular proverb quotes Akpauche, that when you closely inspect the position of the arrow with which his brother killed an antelope, it throws up two options: skilled marksmanship or criminal coveting of another man's game."

"Whichever way it is, Afam has suddenly turned into a national celebrity. He is no longer like one of us. Luck has lifted him to a higher ground."

"With all that rascality about him, he has cleverly escaped the realities that always marked the path of the sluggard."

"Don't you see the joy of his father? The old man had earlier written Afam off as a blockhead. He had consistently lamented that his only regret was that he had no child other than Afam."

"That's it! Success has many friends, but failure is an orphan. See that same father of his as he proudly dances, grinning at every man who looks his way. A few days back, he would tell you that Afam was the only problem he had. Today, that same Afam is becoming the chief cornerstone."

"That is it. May good things happen to us so that we can be celebrated."

The dialogue continued while the mass lasted. Up front, Afamefuna occupied a special seat. He was the special guest of honour that day. When called upon to give a brief testimony, he chose to follow the path he had seen several godly men tread.

Rising from his seat, he started off with a song:

It's not by power

It's not by power

It's not by might

It's not by might

By my spirit says the Lord

This mountain ...

... must be removed

This mountain ...

... must be removed

This mountain ...

... must be removed

By my spirit says the Lord.

"Praise the Lord!" he shouted.

"Halleluiah!" the congregation answered.

"Brethren," Afam continued, "I give God all the glory. I was only praying to pass that examination. I did not know that God had something better for me. When a child is blessed with a gift too big for him, he asks questions to reassure himself he was not misappropriating what is meant for another."

"Praise the Lord!" Ejegerekwu, his mother, shouted, springing to her feet and sitting down again, betraying some joyful emotion.

"Halleluiah!" the congregation answered again.

"I was saying that God had a pleasant surprise for me," Afam continued.

"I am aware that some people had written me off before now. Today, God is reassuring me that he did not write me off. While I thank the Lord for his mercies, I also want to use this medium to advise my fellow young ones not to give up on their pursuits in life."

As soon as the church service was over, all roads led to Justice Ezedinaobi's residence. The legal luminary had made some advance preparations to entertain well-wishers at his residence that afternoon. Several guests wondered why a man of Ezedinaobi's calibre would make so much fuss about an examination as unimportant as that. He was an accomplished man in his own right. A retired justice of the Supreme Court of Nigeria, he was unarguably of the finest breed of erudite legal scholars ever produced by the country. When he retired from active practice, he chose to settle down in Oguta, his village. Many, therefore, could not understand why such a man should attach so much importance to such examination success of a son.

Towards the end of the ceremony, Justice Ezedinaobi informed his guests about the real reasons behind his unusual joy. He was the only son of his late parents, he said; and that he got married while yet a student because his parents were eager to see him become a father. They had been worried that in the unlikely event of Ezedinaobi's demise, the family lineage would be wiped out. However, that early marriage could not produce the result it was intended to produce. The couple could not have a child until twenty-five years after their marriage, long after the death of Ezedinaobi's parents. He chose the name Afamefuna, meaning "may my lineage not be wiped off", in deference to the wish of his parents.

After the birth of Afamefuna, Ezedinaobi and his wife could not have any more children. Since they were educated themselves, they thought it worthy to give Afam the best education they could afford. Being a patriotic Nigerian, Ezedinaobi resisted all the temptation to send his child to the United Kingdom to acquire the best of western education. However, when it came to intellectual development, young Afam could not really be said to be a chip off the old block. His father's judgment was that Afam was intellectually bankrupt and academically dull. Ezedinaobi was therefore surprised and elated when it was confirmed that his son had come through with flying colours. Initially, it sounded incredible to Ezedinaobi. This was because he was previously on the verge of losing all hope. A repeat broadcast of that news item did the magic of convincing Ezedinaobi.

At the proper time, Afamefuna was admitted into the Faculty of Law, University of Calabar, Nigeria to pursue a degree program in criminal law. Before resumption, the faculty authorities looked forward to receiving him. He was already being celebrated. It was the custom of universities to closely monitor students who showed early signs of brilliance, with a view to encouraging such students to seek the path of academic excellence. Moreover, the fact that Afam would enjoy dual full scholarship was an added advantage.

Among his fellow students, Afam was regarded as a goldfish. He was quite agreeable. He mixed freely and was at home with everybody. His comportment in the school was excellent. However, his first semester at the University unveiled the man behind the mask. His performance in the seven courses he took was rather abysmal. From the continuous assessment tests through the first semester examinations, Afam's scripts were a far cry from those of an average student. He could not even attain the borderline position in any paper.

Initially, every lecturer was at a loss, assuming that there must have been a mistake somewhere. One lecturer after another invited Afam to a personal interview to find out the possible immediate and remote causes of such early deterioration. The department arranged for him to see a psychologist who painstakingly took him through some mental drilling and mind-searching to detect possible traces of psycho-analytical imbalance.

Having taken these steps and being satisfied that Afam was mentally sound and emotionally balanced, the department transferred the case to the faculty of law. The faculty, in turn, thoroughly investigated the case and formally reported it to the senate of the school. The senate, thereafter, invited Afam to have an interview session with them. In attendance were the vice-chancellor, the deputy vice-chancellors (academic and administration), the university registrar, and deans of various faculties.

"Good evening, Mr Afamefuna Ezedinaobi," began Professor Uba Babayaro, the dean of the faculty of law.

"Good evening, lady and gentlemen," Afamefuna responded.

"We believe you are aware of the reason we convened this meeting?" the registrar, Dr Felix Ekpo asked.

"I guess I do; but you shall do well to confirm my guess," Afamefuna stated.

"Well, it's because of your poor academic performance," the *Vice*-Chancellor, Professor Peter Offiong confirmed. "The entire system is concerned."

"Concerned?" Afam quietly asked himself. He could not understand why all these distinguished academics could get concerned about the poor performance of just one student among thousands of other students. Memories of events in the secondary school he attended were yet very fresh in his mind. He could vividly remember how some academic staff of that school taunted students who were finding it difficult to cope with some subjects. Such students were called all sorts of names. The students were also in the habit of fighting fire with fire. Every teacher was given a derogatory name by the students. Only a few students saw teachers as partners in progress. The majority concluded that teachers were cruel taskmasters. For many of them, going through the school system was an encumbrance; it was an unnecessary burden laid on them as a result of the conspiratorial agreement between the government and their parents.

Afam was convinced that it was not so with these university dons. They were different. They showed great care and concern. As those questions were being asked, Afam lowered his head. His face looked downward as if he was observing something of interest on the polished floor of the senate conference room. Then he looked up again, quickly surveying the entire room, at a glance seeing everyone present. He summoned up some courage and chose to look at the vice-chancellor directly. To Afam, the vice-chancellor was the head of this team. Afam was impressed with that rare leadership quality of the old professor. The old professor's face truly portrayed his concern. Afam was touched that men with whom he had no personal relationship could show such empathy and care.

"There's yet hope for this country," he muttered to himself.

The vice-chancellor was bespectacled. His eyes seemed to bulge out beyond those glass frames. The far end of his nostrils provided support for those glasses, enabling the professor of trigonometry to see directly with his eyes and read with the aid of the glasses.

"Mr Ezedinaobi," the Registrar called. "I hope you are ready for this exercise. You paint the picture of a man whose mind is very far from here."

"I am with you, sir!" Afam reaffirmed. "With due respect, sir, you may wish to continue," he bowed, addressing the vice-chancellor.

"The pre-admission information we had on you pointed to the possibility of you being a student of exceptional academic brilliance," the registrar noted. "However, your rather poor performance rattled every one of us. That's the reason why we decided to invite you, have an interactive session with you, and possibly find ways to help you get moving again."

"For us to be able to meaningfully assist you, we'd advise that you answer every question sincerely," the dean of the faculty of education counselled. "Now, tell us, what is the problem?"

The apparent display of love and genuine concern by these men and women fuelled Afamefuna's resolve to let the senate into every detail of his journey to the university. He was touched and acted accordingly.

"I would request that you all exercise some good degree of patience, listen to me, and only then decide on what to do," Afam began.

"Go ahead; we shall all listen to you," the vice-chancellor assured him.

"By way of introduction," Afamefuna began, "I sincerely wish to thank every one of you. I am really impressed with such rare displays of altruism on your part. What I am witnessing today gives me the blessed assurance that this country, our country, my country, has a future. It indicates that there is still hope for my generation and generations of Nigerians yet unborn.

"I am a Nigerian born in this age. I belong to the generation of Nigerians who have perfectly learnt that the end justifies the means. Whilst not making any excuses or justifying myself and my generation, I dare say that what we are engaged in today is totally based on what we have seen the larger society do. Every man is expected to dance to the music of his time. That might as well explain the general trend among the youth of this country.

"My father is not only responsible but respectable. He is held in the very highest esteem. My parents are well educated. With the highest sense of humility, the name of Justice Innocent Ejemeoru Ezedinaobi is well known all over the country. That man is my father. I am his only son. I am his only child! My parents tried to give me the best education money could afford. However, they also wanted to have me around them all the time. My father particularly believed that it would be a better way to moulding me in character and in learning.

"Ladies and gentlemen, my father was abruptly retired from service. His alleged victimization stemmed from a minority judgment he delivered on an electoral case. Pardon me for this digression. That issue is not our interest here. However, that retirement affected a whole lot of things. It dramatically altered the course of our lives. The family decided to relocate to the village. Due to my father's patriotic zeal for everything Nigerian, and his desire to closely monitor my development, he got me transferred to a secondary school in my village.

"In that school, I was idolized. It was a public school. Children from rich and middle-class homes were always sent to comparatively better schools in the cities and overseas. The spirit of patriotism that ran through my father was the vehicle that drove me to that village school. Without being ready for it, I saw that I was obviously being given some privileges. Both teachers and students gave me some preferential treatment. That was not the case in my former school at Abuja. There, everybody was somebody. Nobody really cared who 'your parents or guardians are. Any misconduct was extensively investigated and lovingly corrected.

"While in the village school, I also noticed that I could do just about anything and get away with it. Willy-nilly, I began to retrogress. I also began to closely associate with a group of students who rated themselves as being above the rest; not that they were academically brighter than others, but that they had succeeded at getting others to accept that they were powerful and influential enough to do anything and escape the wrath of the law. They readily welcomed me into their group.

"Other students dared not challenge us openly. We were on very friendly terms with a lot of teachers. During school hours, we could choose to pursue some other interests. It did not matter to us when we missed our classes because we knew we could always get ourselves out of any trouble. Gradually, I seriously began to lose interest in industry and education. Seeing the development of some ex-students of the college, who trod that path before us, helped to further strengthen our crooked ways. Some of them were in various universities. A few were gainfully employed. In our discussions, we always tried to devise means to achieve cheap success.

"News emanating from the political front also confirmed our philosophy that one does not need to work diligently to get to the top in our country. We perfectly understood that there were three things needed most by anyone aspiring to authority and fame in our country. We identified these three things as natural intelligence, the right connections, and some financial backing for inducement and settlements when such are needed. You would agree with me that no one is certain of the academic qualifications of the present crop of political leaders in our country.

"Inwardly, I did not really enjoy such exclusive privileges. On the surface, I enjoyed the privileged status, but there was an inner voice of reason and restraint prodding me to change. A few times, I strongly desired to share these with my father, but I was afraid that he could take it to the extreme. Yet, no matter how much I desired to change and engage in a more fulfilling and honourable lifestyle, I saw myself falling deeper and deeper into that horrible pit of dishonour. I was enslaved by criminal passion and crooked mentality.

"Among my friends, however, there was a twist. The emotional and moral conflict in me began to look for a physical outlet to be expressed. My friends soon noticed the sudden drop in my level of commitment and enthusiasm. Every one of them branded me a weakling with a chicken heart, saying that if I continued that way, I wouldn't amount to any success. They mentioned names of several bigwigs in our country about whom the press had dug up one scandalous issue or another. Yet, all those ones continued to be relevant in our society.

"One of them even alluded to my father's victimization as being the result of his refusal to be bought over with money. He said that those who were obviously in the wrong about that matter were still very much around the corridors of power. Finally, he warned that if I chose to tread that same way of my father, the very best I could hope for would be an empty national honour with poverty as a garland.

"All that they said sounded like truth. Our country was awash with news of the shameful and greedy ways of political office-holders. From that moment, I wholly gave myself to the guiding philosophy of the group. We saw ourselves as truants with a focus. For our admission examinations, we all identified villages with examination centres popular among candidates for examination malpractice. We had an agent who came from a neighbouring state to solicit for entry of candidates. The beautifully encouraging thing about what he did was that he had a wide network of schools that worked with him. The schools were at different localities. He would distribute candidates to these centres as he deemed fit. He was an extraordinary agent.

"He charged close to six times the original registration fee. I had no problem paying since my mother was my very close friend. I let her know everything I did. She sponsored my payment. I was doubly registered, switching the positions of my first and middle names, while maintaining my surname. Part of the money we paid was used to bribe supervisors and examiners. The cost of logistics had to be taken care of also. It was stated in the contract that it was his obligation to convey us to the examination centre and take us back to Oguta at the end of the day. Naturally, the agent ought to make some handsome profit for his role. It was a well-syndicated arrangement. From then on, we could boast to other students that we were certain of placement into universities in the next academic year. I also knew my chances were double.

"Surely, we patronized him. We rated him as excellent, so we all paid the fees he demanded. It was then his lot to meet with proprietors and principals of the various schools earmarked for the exercise, discuss with them, and have us registered accordingly. He registered us by proxy. On that fateful day, our agent was punctual enough. He arrived at Oguta in a hired bus which was stationed across the lake, on part of the countryside. Every student who was a part of this arrangement had to gather at Kalabari Beach. Here, we boarded that bus and took off to the examination centre. My mother had also arranged to be at Kregani, the community in which we were scheduled to sit the examinations. She drove all alone in a private car to Kregani, communicating with me all the way as she drove down.

"That was the day my eyes were opened to see the reasons behind the outcry by concerned Nigerians that our education sector was comatose, and the system rotten. I witnessed first-hand the rot that has become the education sector. Everybody in that hall, including law enforcement agents, was part of the fraudulent design. Answers were dictated for every candidate to note. In each paper, seventy percent of the answers were dictated, leaving each candidate to personally attend to the remaining thirty percent. Truly, I could not satisfactorily answer one of those remaining questions. I left that hall unhappy.

"Meanwhile, while we were sitting for this examination at one centre, my mother was with the agent, sorting out issues at the other centre where I was registered. There, both agreed to meet at a remote hotel in town. Later in the day, that meeting took place. The four of us, which comprised my mother, the agent, a young undergraduate from one of the universities and myself, were in attendance. The young undergraduate helped us to answer the questions. I had to personally fill the sheets and enter the answers as agreed by all. We were quite certain of the answers as we had some textbooks to consult. The young undergraduate was handsomely paid.

"At the end of that exercise, I was happy. I was satisfied, having enough faith that the possibility of my being admitted into the university was rather high. I thought it was all over, but my mother thought otherwise. She believed whatever was being done must be done perfectly. She believes in leaving no stone unturned in her quest to accomplish tasks she set for herself. She mapped out her road to further accomplishing her set target. On our way back to Oguta that evening, my mother told me that the journey had just begun.

"How do you mean, Mum?" I asked.

"I advise you to wait and see," she answered. "Once I am through, I'll let you know." I, therefore, let her be, knowing that whatever she was planning, I would be the principal beneficiary. A fortnight afterwards, my mother informed me that she had travelled to the headquarters of the Joint Admissions Bureau in Abuja, where she perfected the strategy. It was only then that she could assure that the issue of my admission was already concluded; that the main issue for consideration was the points to be assigned to me. She was certain that the gentleman she had met was highly impressed with the gratification he got from her. While all this was happening, my father was ignorant. My mother and I knew that if my father got to know about our plans, they would be totally foiled. He wouldn't do a thing to discredit the family name. He cherished his reputation and would do everything that was right to protect it.

"Ladies and gentlemen, I guess you are beginning to understand why I earlier stated that what my generation is enmeshed in reflects the rot in the larger society. We have tried to copy the older generations, and possibly surpass their performance level in the area of being intelligent and smart. When the results were finally released, I was not disappointed. Some of the candidates who sat for that examination with me wondered how I managed to scale through. The results of the centre where I physically sat the examination were cancelled, but the other results were released, including mine. That is my story. Thank you."

"That's a pretty amazing piece of testimony!" the vice-chancellor remarked.

"I would have considered that rather incredible but for the fact that it came directly from the horse's mouth," Professor Rotimi added.

"Mr Ezedinaobi," the vice-chancellor addressed Afam. "We really thank you for your very frank and detailed exposition. By this testimony, you have helped to broaden our knowledge on methodologies of examination malpractice. That might as well be where we'll draw the curtain with you today. You may wish to leave now. We promise to get back to you as soon as possible. Good evening!"

As Afam left, the vice-chancellor addressed members of the senate.

"Ladies and gentlemen," he began. "It is obvious that we have an uncommon situation at hand. It calls for a thorough brainstorming to arrive at a very reasonable decision. Do you all agree with me?"

"Not exactly, sir!" Professor Okeakwukwo, the dean of the faculty of education said. "With due respect, sir, I want to remind everybody present, in case we have forgotten; that the university has an existing policy on examination malpractice and intellectual fraud. I wonder if there is anything about this matter that calls for brainstorming. We ought to implement that policy; otherwise, we shall not only be setting a bad precedent but also be encouraging mediocrity and unwittingly lowering academic standards here."

"Not so, Professor Okeakwukwo," Dr Isemin corrected. He was the dean of the faculty of social sciences. He continued, "I believe the V.C. has not derailed. I share his views that this case is rather isolated and challenging. We carry a moral burden - the burden of treating this matter with the strictness and seriousness it requires, as other cases before it have been treated, and at the same time demonstrating enough solidarity with Afam for standing by the truth and testifying against a fraudulent system in which he was the principal beneficiary."

"We must be very careful," Professor Roselyn Ntuyang cautioned. "The decision we take today shall be weighed on the scale of equity. It would definitely become a reference point in the future."

"Could we please move forward and make contributions towards arriving at a decision?" the vice-chancellor advised.

"It's simple!" Professor Usen declared. "I agree with Professor Okeakwukwo's contribution that the young man should be rusticated. That position is in line with the policies and by-laws of the university."

"Outright rustication may do more harm than good," Dr Isemin corrected. "I suggest we give him some probationary status."

"How do you mean?" the vice-chancellor asked, directing his question at Isemin. "Could you please properly expatiate on this?"

"I am considering a novel approach wherein we agree with him to get him suspended from the department, while at the same time retaining his right to the university hostel and other facilities. While still being a part of the university community, he'd properly enter for the senior secondary school certificate examination and be registered with a private tutorial school for intensive coaching. If he scales through that hurdle, we lift the suspension and allow him to continue his program."

"That sounds very reasonable to me," the vice-chancellor said. "But the floor is still open for more suggestions."

"What would other students and the entire university community think of us?" Professor Okeakwukwo asked, maintaining his earlier stance. "Questions must arise as to why we treated this case with an overdose of leniency. There might then be insinuations that we have become part of the rot everybody is talking about, yet nobody seems ready to confront."

"That's exactly my concern here," Professor Usen noted. "In any given situation, transparency is a strong shield against the arrows of uninformed public criticism."

"On my part, I see enough merit in the argument put forward by Dr Isemin," Professor Roselyn Ntuyang stated. "We rarely have students who forthrightly relate issues about themselves based on their convictions that their acts were immoral and criminal. I, therefore, suggest that we adopt that recommendation to encourage the reign of truth."

"The fact that by the time the results of the proposed examinations are out, the student in question would have lost an academic session should serve as enough deterrent to him," Dr Isemin said, reinforcing his position.

"In that case, what happens with the dual scholarship he enjoys and his listing on the Joint Admissions hall of fame?" asked Professor Rotimi. "If we eventually retain him on probation, it would be ethically obligatory for us to inform sponsors of these scholarships and the admissions board. When such is eventually done, what basis do we use to allow him to continue his program next session?"

"That's a pretty intelligent question, Professor Rotimi," Dr Isemin answered. "The university enjoys some autonomy. That shall not be a problem in any way."

"Dr Isemin, I guess you have missed the mark here," Professor Rotimi pointed out. "We don't have to abuse the right of autonomy. The young man in question engaged in the highest degree of examination malpractice. Since we intend to advise him to sit for the senior secondary school certificate examination, we had better ask him to also sit for the joint admissions examinations. The university could then liaise with the examination bodies to treat his case especially, ensuring his results would be urgently processed and released."

"I personally agree with Professor Rotimi," said Professor Graham, who was making his very first contribution to the deliberations. "I suggest we fuse this into the main suggestions of Dr Isemin and develop a blueprint for the project. When that is done, it would be a win-win situation."

The senate explored different options, thoroughly analysing the merits and demerits of each option. Anyone who had an opinion had ample opportunity to offer such. At the end, the argument put forward by Dr Isemin, as amended with contributions from Professor Rotimi, was formally adopted. The following day, Afamefuna was invited and informed of the position of the senate. Part of that decision was that the senate would call a press conference and make the position of the university known to the public. This, the vice-chancellor said, was to avoid baseless rumour, suspicion, and misinterpretation within and outside the university community.

CHAPTER 8.
ELEVEN SEVENTEEN

The venue was Force Headquarters Annex, Moloney Street, Obalende, Lagos. The security arrangement was rather extraordinary. Security was beefed up to forestall any embarrassing interference from men of the underworld. The Police high command led by the Assistant Inspector-General in charge of Zone 1 was billed to address a press conference on the menace of armed robbery in the zone. Simultaneously, some suspected armed robbers would be paraded. Images of the suspects would be beamed live on television screens across the country. Fierce-looking mobile policemen were strategically positioned all over the Force Headquarters' Annex. The police also cordoned off a section of Moloney Street, which in effect created terrible traffic situations around the ever-busy Obalende.

Itinerant traders, drivers, bus conductors, and several tens of thousands of people conduct their business in or pass through Obalende every day. Besides its position as a leading contender for the prize of the busiest spot in Nigeria, Obalende also holds a distinguished grapevine status - distinguished in the sense that much of the rumour emanating from here always turns out to be true, not mere speculations. Obalende's place becomes more strategic in the light of its geographical positioning and triangular web-structure: connecting Lagos Island - joint headquarters of corporate Nigeria, and of Nigeria's most dreaded social miscreants, otherwise called area boys, with Ikoyi - home to top government functionaries, high-ranking members of the diplomatic community, industrial and business chiefs, and Victoria Island - an interesting combination of typologies of peoples and practices of Lagos Island and Ikoyi. Obalende remains important, both to the bourgeoisie and the common man in Lagos.

There are a few features very unique to the Nigeria Police. One such feature is their tradition of praising themselves and singing their accomplishments. Another is their unwillingness, non-preparedness, and ineffectiveness to respond to distress calls from the civil populace whenever the latter is endangered. Today, policemen are about beating their chests to declare the successful burst of a crime syndicate. Flanked by top Police chiefs from the state, the Assistant Inspector-General, Mr Nuhu Ifamuyiwa began:

"Gentlemen of the press, the Nigeria Police wishes to alert all law-abiding citizens and residents of our beloved country that a new dimension has been added to criminal activities by bad eggs in the society. No matter what tactics they employ, however, we are ever ready and willing to trace them to their hide-outs, smoke them out of those holes, and bring them to face the laws of the land.

"It is indeed disheartening that otherwise honourable men and women are today teaming up with base criminals to unleash a reign of terror on innocent and law-abiding citizens. These wicked and unreasonable men always leave in their wake bloodbaths, sorrow and anguish. By their acts, they are turning our beloved country into a theatre of violent crime. This, by implication, could suggest to genuine entrepreneurs and potential foreign investors that our country is no longer safe for business. When such horrific pictures are painted of our country, and further ingrained on the psyches of the peoples of the world, the outcome would impact very negatively and seriously, both on our socio-political state and the economic development of our country. It would indeed be far-reaching.

"Bearing this in mind, coupled with the strong support and co-operation we have been receiving from the President of the Federal Republic of Nigeria, we emphatically and categorically state that the age of sacred cow syndrome is over. We shall ruthlessly deal with criminals of whatever extraction or class.

"Today, we also wish to parade before you all, the entire nation, and indeed the world, a gang of suspected armed robbers, representative of the new crime order we earlier enunciated. Making up this team are four women and thirteen men. They come from different professional and occupational backgrounds: bankers, serving police personnel, private businessmen and women, and others who seem not to be engaged in anything other than crime. From our investigations, their major targets have been banks. Occasionally also, they attack operators of bureau de change outfits at different locations.

"Gentlemen, we parade the following persons before you all today: A.S.P Asari Woke; A.S.P. Adamu Musa; Sergeant Bassey Effiom and Corporal Njoku Nwite - all serving police officers and men. We parade before you, Miss Ify Uyammadu; Miss Eneobong Ebri; Mr Osaze Okunzua; Mr Taiwo Olopade; Miss Nike Olumoren; and Malam Shehu Muktar - staff of different banks in the country. Others include Ms Princess Igbinoba - the proprietor of Princess Sleek Restaurant, Ahmed Onibudu, Victoria Island; Mr Essien Imoh, a driver and mechanic; Mr Esumejuya Okene; Mr Amos Jalingo; Mr Iyorchia Nandev; Mr Okoro Nnanna;

and Dr Akinfenwa Olona - all being core operational members of this well-run robbery syndicate."

As the police chief read out each name, the suspect so named is shoved forward by a policeman standing behind him or her. Most of the suspects tried in vain to evade the capture of various cameras facing them. Their faces betrayed different emotions. Some seemed to be sincerely repentant for engaging in crime. Some were indifferent to the situation in which they found themselves. A few others were totally defiant and did not care what would become of them. One of these defiant ones was Amos Jalingo. The son of a retired infantry soldier, Amos's childhood could be better said to have been spent in Nigeria. A product of a forced relationship between his Jukun father and his prisoner-of-war mother of Igbo extraction, Amos was born in Igboland in the course of Igbo subjugation during the Nigerian civil war. He spent much of his infanthood with his parents who traversed the entire then Eastern region prosecuting the war to preserve the unity of Nigeria.

Amos was barely eighteen months old when the Biafrans surrendered. However, that decision to surrender did not change anything with regards to little Amos's father's frequent travels. As the father was being transferred from one military formation to another, Amos was growing up in diverse cultural landscapes in Nigeria. Life in the barracks for a growing Nigerian boy was not particularly good for building character. Discipline, which often characterized the institution of the army, was ironically lacking among children and dependents of soldiers who lived in the barracks. Besides the squalid environmental conditions and poor physical infrastructure, the barracks seemed to be a haven for such scoundrels as pickpockets, petty thieves, and social misfits, provided they never committed such crimes within the barracks. *'Bloody civilians'* as they were often referred to were allowed into the barracks only if accompanied by a soldier or his dependent. Otherwise, he would be thoroughly searched and properly interrogated before he was permitted entry. Amos grew up under these conditions.

While in Command Secondary School, Ibadan, Amos took an alias for himself. He told his friends that he preferred being called "Boldface". Severally, he was rusticated from school. The same number of times, his father got him back into school. Now Amos's father had been transferred to Port Harcourt, Rivers State. The father's frequent transfers also helped to obliterate Amos's rather unenviable records. It would be wrong to say that the young boy did not change. He truly changed, but he obviously changed for the worse. Every passing day, he was gaining more knowledge, diabolic knowledge, so to say.

In those days, if a soldier in Nigeria was counted as lost, he was an oddity, eternally lost to the perfidy of riotous and sensual living. A soldier was the Nigerian sacrificial lamb. In any case, you don't expect such men to come home with responsible offspring, if any offspring at all. There really was no time for a khaki spotting soldier to play the role of a responsible father in the twin fields of social and moral tutelage. He ordinarily had no time; not when he needed more time for drinking bouts and frequent frolicking with women of easy virtue; women whose supply was over-abundant. As a soldier, Jalingo believed his whole duty was to feed, clothe and shelter his family. Secondarily, he'd pick up bills for their formal education also. Jalingo was also of the opinion that moral nurture of children was better left in the jurisdiction of their mother.

In Port Harcourt, Amos extended his circle of friendship beyond Bori camp, the army barracks in the city. He had many friends at the waterside. Mile 3 through Mile 1 area and beyond made up their constituency. There is an area popularly known as *"man must whack"*, an indirect reference to the jungle-style operation of residents there. *Man must whack* was a sort of melting pot for their rendezvous. Here, he met a young man of similar nature. Within a short while, a very strong bond was established between Amos Jalingo and Asari Woke. That bond was stronger than the love of a man for a woman. They had more than one thing in common. Despite their apparent rascality, Boldface and Asari, "the hawk", were both determined to acquire a university education. Though they always engaged in street fights and gangsterism, both young men found time to pursue their dream of going through the university system.

Having established some sources of continuous cash flow into their coffers, they did not find it difficult to pay "mercenaries" who entered for University Matriculation Examinations on their behalf, and subsequently sat those examinations and came out with good grades. Both gained admission into the University of Nigeria, Nsukka. Amos was offered a BSc. programme in the Department of Soil Sciences, while Asari secured admission into the Department of Sociology and Anthropology. With a rock-solid foundational base in thuggery, thievery and violence, both felt at home joining the most dreaded campus cult in Nsukka. "De Devil's Advocates" were the undisputed leaders in cult activities in that university community.

Both Asari and Amos believed that every enterprise that should succeed is structured for and aimed at continuous improvement. For the duo, excellence is the ability to consistently make a stunning success of a chosen path. The path of honour and glory, therefore, may lead to excellence. The path of dishonour and depravity may equally lead to excellence. The latter was the path chosen by Amos and Asari. They successfully sold their conviction to some of their colleagues in 'De Devil's Advocates'. As a watchword, they adopted a popular saying; "be the best of what you are".

Within and outside the campus environment, Asari and Amos continued to fine-tune their plans to float and run a formidable, high-profile, largely networked armed robbery syndicate. They agreed that to run such an outfit was not going to be a very easy task. Both "the Hawk" and "Boldface" were no strangers to crime. They began as independent pickpockets and street fighters. While in Port Harcourt, the garden city, both were errand boys to some political heavyweights in Rivers state. They were known for their effectiveness at mobilizing young men of identical socio-political persuasion, who were used as pawns to wage bloody wars on political opponents. Anyone who was considered a threat to the electoral success of their paymasters was an enemy.

Before graduating to that level, they had been largely responsible for the stealing and receiving of stolen cell phones. Boys who worked under them were obliged to report every operation, successful or not.

Reporting of such helped them appraise the effectiveness of the approaches employed. Besides the field workers who carried out the actual thefts, there were vigilante group members whose duty it was to monitor the operational environment, as well as serve as checks on those field workers who might want to be funny. It would not be an overstatement to say that this group was responsible for over fifty percent of all mobile phones stolen in the garden city.

It was from this group that "the Hawk" and "Boldface" recruited the boys for political thuggery. At that level of political jobbery, they were responsible for blackmail, intimidation, physical assault, assassination of opponents as well as masterminding election-rigging on a massive scale. In fact, Asari and Jalingo were the de facto leaders of organized crime in the then Rivers state. Part of the reason they eventually chose to acquire further education was to enhance their socio-political profile. They were dreaming of picking up political appointments or running for elective offices later in their lives.

While in the university, however, the young men discovered something in 'De Devil's Advocates'. They found, in that cult group, an avenue for expression of their real selves. Both felt that meeting their self-imposed financial obligations was little or no task.

After all, they continued to enjoy political patronage considered commensurate with their status. However, that did not last very long. Their paymasters evolved a method of systematic reduction of the patronage and privileges the duo enjoyed. New super-kids had taken over control of organized crime and violence in Rivers state. Politicians who had earlier favoured the Hawk and Boldface also analysed the implications of continuing to patronize the duo to the exclusion of those who were mostly physically present in the state. Some of the boys who were the duo's lieutenants declared that they had equally come of age themselves. With firearms and other dangerous weapons in their possession, they dared to stamp their authority as the reigning kings of terror in the state.

Boldface and the Hawk were not bothered by these developments. They perfectly understood the laws of the jungle: survival of the fittest. They had always played that game. Being fully convinced that they could not possibly have their cake and eat it, they channelled their entire energy into activities in the university, and Nsukka in general. Channelling their activities there meant much more than engaging in academic and cult activities. Besides their involvement in 'De Devil's Advocates', the duo and their team occasionally mounted roadblocks at various spots not only on Enugu-Onitsha expressway but also on Enugu-Nsukka-Obollo

Afor road. Armed robbery operations became a very effective alternative to political thuggery, at least for as long as money was involved.

With the proceeds from their several escapades, they had no problem financing their educational pursuits as well as meeting their obligations to 'De Devil's Advocates'. For purposes of more effective coordination of their activities, they rented a two-bedroom apartment in downtown Onuiyi. That was at the beginning of their third year at university. They became known in the university community as "the Dons".

The Joint Admissions and Matriculation Board (JAMB) was the regulatory agency responsible for the admission of students into Nigerian universities. JAMB had its criteria for offering prospective students' provisional admission into schools of their choice. Every university also had its own requirements for every academic discipline spelt out in the brochure. But the duo, through their group, had made themselves formidable forces at determining the successful stay or otherwise of many students in the university.

Any member of 'De Devil's Advocates whose friend or relation is murdered dare not fight back if the offensive came via a fellow advocate. The early initiation process always took them to Okija shrine in Ihiala Local Government Area of Anambra State. At the shrine, they all swore an oath of secrecy and total protection of one another. Sharp razor blades were used to lacerate the skin of members. Blood was shed from everyone into a central pool. Afterwards, the blood is mingled with wine and passed round for everyone to have a sip. This way, every member is made to believe in the depth and efficacy of the bond and brotherhood of the group. Injury inflicted on a member is injury inflicted on all. The same blood, they assume, flowed through the veins of every member. Confirmed betrayal of one or more members of De Devil's Advocates by another is the only reason for which the cult could harm or out-rightly eliminate a member.

Asari, "the Hawk", and Boldface adopted this practice in the recruitment of members of the robbery gang for immediate and future operations. Other members included Adamu Musa of the Department of Political Science; Osazua Okunzua of the Department of Economics; Taiwo Olopade, Shehu Muktar, and Esumejuya Okene, all of the Animal Science Department; and Iyorchia Nandev and Okoro Nnanna, both of whom were of the Department of Geography. The choice of these additional seven persons was very carefully done. The Hawk and Boldface knew that those seven were popular with all other members of De Devil's Advocates. They were known for the dispatch with which they often executed assignments. They were bold and brazen-faced at meting out cruelty to supposedly deserving victims. To crown it all, they always enjoyed working together. To other members, they were known as "the swift seven".

Two ladies were informally drafted into the team. Ify Uyammadu was the first-choice girlfriend of Asari Woke, while Eneobong Ebri was Amos Jalingo's confessed lover. Both ladies became members willy-nilly. At an event that could best pass as the inaugural meeting of the gang, there was a no holds barred interactive session held at the insistence of Boldface. The venue of that meeting was the duo's apartment at Onuiyi. All doors and windows were shut to minimize distractions and intrusion from unwanted elements.

"My guys!" Amos began. "You are all aware of the reason for convening this all-important meeting. We want to birth a new group - a movement that'll ensure our continued socio-political and economic survival in this nation. Others may wish to call us armed robbers. They may call us criminals. But we know we are only fighting for the survival of our souls; fighting to keep body and soul together."

"Is that the reason why we came to school?" Esumejuya Okene queried.

"Esu! Calm down! Listen to Boldface and get the project outlay and the justification for it before your questions," the Hawk counselled.

"Okay, my guys," Amos continued. "It does not bother me and shall not bother me whenever anybody says anything about my being a criminal. Who is not a criminal in this country? Is it the occupant of the number-one seat in the country, or the so-called federal and state lawmakers? Tell me, are the federal ministers and state commissioners free from crime? Do you intend to exonerate heads of departments and top functionaries of this government? Tell me, who among them can cast the first stone of accusation? They may not handle firearms and waylay road users; they may not invade banks and forcefully cart away huge sums of money in the full glare of the public, but they do worse things than these.

"Are you all not aware that the ruling party, the National Democratic Alliance has earned itself the sobriquet *share the money?* Is it not because of the reckless abandon with which they share monthly allocations from the federation account? They all share these monies among themselves without regard to the poor state of physical infrastructure in this country. Nobody thinks of the state of total decay that has become the hallmark of our so-called citadels of learning. What about the issue of healthcare delivery? Don't we have ill-equipped and under-funded teaching hospitals scattered all over the country?

"Today, we are all in school pursuing one academic programme or the other. When we graduate, only heaven knows how many decades each of us will have to wait before he gets a well-paid job. Our universities continue to produce graduates while the government has no policy in place to ensure the creation of jobs for this teeming and ever-increasing population of real and potential jobseekers. Such high and unregulated increase in the cost of transportation is enough testimony to the total neglect our roads have suffered over the years.

"My guys! These men send their children to the best schools overseas, funded with the money they steal daily from our national till. They tax our poor parents. They drill oil from our soil. This, they sell to the West, stash the bulk of the money into personal foreign accounts, and condemn us and the entire citizenry to live in the agony of perpetual servitude. Ever since we grew up to hear of our country being referred to as a third world nation, that third world tag has never left us. This is not because we do not make enough money to better the lots of our countrymen, but because a few greedy men have turned themselves into a cabal who control what happens in our country.

"It is my considered opinion, our opinion, that we, as bona fide citizens of our great country, are eminently qualified to receive our share of the national cake. This cake has been baked by Mother Nature for us all. We shall not be doing justice to nature if we continue to demonstrate apathy while a few elements whose minds, warped as they are, arrogate to themselves ownership of, and monopoly to share this cake as they will.

"If the good things that are assumed the rights of every citizen in well-governed nations elude us, we shall go and get them ourselves. To fold our hands and suffer the same injustice that our immediate parents suffered and are currently suffering, is to guarantee the same suffering for our children yet unborn. We shall all take our table knives and cut our share of this cake. We do not have direct access to the federal treasury and state funds, but we can masterfully target the banks. You may not know, but it is not far from the truth that over eighty percent of commercial banks operating in this country are owned by these same men who control our political destiny.

"Henceforth, every one of us, even before graduation, shall effectively plan towards serving with the police, or with any commercial bank. You cannot operate successfully in these banks without insiders who provide information on the movement of cash. The police connection is for reduction of risks in our envisaged future operations, and as an alternative source of weapons. When we infiltrate the police and banks, then it becomes easier for us to hit gold. My guys! This is our considered methodology for evenly spreading financial empowerment and economic emancipation. Contributions and questions are welcome. Thank you, guys!" He sat down.

The Hawk was the next to stand up. He cleared his throat. Facing Boldface, the Hawk lifted his right hand and gave Boldface the thumbs-up salute. "Congratulations!" he said. "I must say that was a well-articulated speech."

He then turned to the entire house. "You could count on the fingers of one hand the number of our so-called political leaders who could give such a speech with so much convincing logic. As an addendum to that, I'd like to say that we are not interested in wasting human lives. We intend that our operations shall be without a premeditated intention to kill. This we shall try to achieve as much as possible."

"What happens if we are attacked?" asked Nnanna.

"Ah! You don't test the swimming skills of a fish in the river. If you do, you would have only succeeded in sending it back to its natural habitat," the Hawk answered.

"What does that connote in relation to our discussion," Iyorchia probed.

The Hawk further explained; "Whoever dares to test our ability and determination to succeed, let him engage us in shooting. Whenever we are faced with such threat, our resolve shall be to leave nothing alive in that environment. Mark my words! We shall not lose anyone due to carelessness. Our wounded must not be left to the mercy of enemies. When faced with such dangers, our position shall be total recourse to firearms."

"What do we do with security men and police personnel guarding banks?" Shehu asked.

"We shall not operate in any bank without obtaining enough information about that bank. Security operatives guarding a bank shall be overpowered, disarmed, and rendered inactive before every operation commences in earnest."

"How feasible are these plans?" Osazua asked. "We came from different states and may eventually be engaged in one thing or the other at different places," he added.

"Osas!" Boldface answered. "The Hawk and I have already planned towards that. We shall rent a large and comfortable apartment in Lagos. There, everybody shall be welcome until you all find your feet to rent your own apartments. Some of you already have places to stay in Lagos. The only requirement is for everyone to agree that we want to do this, and that the choice of Lagos as an operational base is acceptable to everybody."

"What about basic operational tools?" Iyorchia asked. "I hope you don't expect us to rely on police-type rifles for such high-risk operations."

"The police shall only be a source. We already have access to some. We also have the necessary contact to purchase just about any type of weapon we consider necessary for our operations. Sub-machine guns; Pump-action; AK47 Assault rifles; just name it! We shall not run out of necessary tools. Leave that aspect to Boldface and me," the Hawk said with a note of conviction.

"In the absence of any other business, this meeting shall not be deemed to have ended successfully and on a happy note without item number 7", Boldface suggested.

"Ify, baby!" Asari called.

'Yes, my baby!" Ify Uyammadu answered from the direction of the kitchen. She cat-walked into the living room. Dressed in a pair of crimson-red denim long pants and a black body hug top, she smiled at the visitors. She was well acquainted with every one of them.

"Hi, guys!" she greeted.

"First lady!" they all responded, acknowledging her position in Asari's life.

"What do you have for us?" the Hawk asked. "Everybody is famished."

"What's that supposed to mean?" she fired back, pretending to be annoyed. "Am I your housewife?"

"First lady!" they all hailed again, knowing she was in a happy mood.

"If you are not interested in being the first lady of the Hawk, many girls out there are ready to take over that position," the Hawk countered, in a lighter mood.

"Is the road to this place hidden? Let whoever thinks she is bold enough come and try it. I wouldn't issue empty threats to imaginary persons," she retorted.

"You win!" Boldface intervened.

"I concede," the Hawk added.

"Then ask your question again. Rephrase it and address me properly," Ify insisted.

"Yes, your ladyship!" the Hawk answered, toeing that line. "My lady," he began, "my clients here present are facing serious threats from pangs of hunger. It is my special privilege to inform this honourable court that they are in danger of sudden physical death, cessation of terrestrial powers and soul damnation if good, tasty, mouth-watering and stomach-filling food is not immediately made available to them.

"Pursuant upon this, my lady, I pray that each be abundantly supplied with a meal of remarkable sumptuosity for the purposes of physical nourishment, mental balance, and continued spiritual bliss on earth."

"Court will grant the prayers of the defence counsel," Ify ruled and excused herself. She re-joined Eneobong in the kitchen. Soon, they served everybody an appetizer of fresh fish pepper soup. Following was the main course of pounded yam with edikaikong soup - a special delicacy, native to Eneobong's home state of Cross-river. Then a dessert of local fruit salad was served. Then beer was made available for everyone to drink as he or she wished.

In the very spirit of practising to perfect their skill, the newly formed gang became more active in cult activities in the university, and in robbery operations within the state. Several times, they made incursions into neighbouring states. Before their graduation, they had made some handsome fortunes from their dishonourable business. Armed with the matriculation numbers of all eleven of them, Amos travelled to Abuja for the sole purpose of visiting the headquarters of the National Youth Service Corps. There, he effectively used the weapon of money to lobby for every one of them to be posted to Lagos for their mandatory one-year national youth service exercise.

With money, almost all things are possible in this country.

In Lagos, the game of lobbying for lucrative primary assignment posting became more intensive. There were varied interests. Ify, Eneobong, and Shehu, out of the entire lot, succeeded at being posted to banks. Adamu Musa was posted to the National Population Bureau, Headquarters annexe. The remaining seven corps members got posted to different secondary schools.

Planning is one thing; practical execution of such a plan is another. It was not that easy kick-starting group operations on the envisaged scale as planned. For two years, the gang continued in the familiar turf of highway robbery. Notwithstanding the difficulties and risk of venturing into bank robbery, the gang, spurred on by the Hawk and Boldface, persisted in their vision. They secured a seven-bedroom detached duplex in Idimu, a suburb of Lagos. The choice of Idimu, Boldface had explained, stemmed from its status as a rural community. Not much of the land at Idimu had been developed at the time. Idimu offered the necessary privacy for coordination of their activities. While at Idimu, they also explored illegal routes used by other unpatriotic elements for the smuggling of vehicles between Nigeria and Benin Republic.

It took Adamu Musa three years from the year he completed his youth service exercise to being admitted into the Nigeria Police. The gang made effective use of their network to push one another into positions as previously dreamt. In seven years, they had all been strategically placed. Eneobong Ebri, who continued to be a live-in lover of Boldface, opened the floodgate of bank robbery. Having served her compulsory one-year programme with Forthright Bank and being fortunate enough to be retained by the bank, she initially displayed exceptional commitment and industry. Within six years, she had become an assistant manager in the Foreign Operations Department of the bank. This position gave her the privilege of being adequately informed, not only on the movement of foreign currency in and out of the bank but also on major customers who were involved in these transactions.

Eneobong was obviously well paid. She had even suggested to Amos that they jettison the idea and practice of robbery and face the fulfilling path of honour and industry.

"Why have you suddenly decided to become a turncoat?" Amos asked.

"What reasons do you have to choose an immoral criminal path above honesty and a respectable life?"

"I am amazed at you. Do you mean to say that you have been with me all these years without understanding the basic ingredients that drive my philosophy?"

"I do strongly believe that those ingredients are not strong and reasonable enough to compel us to continue on such a path."

"Well, I am not fighting for the sake of money alone. I am fighting an unjust and lopsided system."

"The same system has offered me a good job. The same system is beckoning you and me to come over and join the tea party."

"Eneobong, listen and listen very carefully. I swear to God!" With his forefinger, he touched the floor of the room, touched his tongue, pointed the finger up to the sky, and continued.

"I swear to God that if you chicken out at this stage, the consequences would be very dire for both of us."

"How do you mean?"

"How do I mean?" he repeated. "Okay! This is what I mean: for close to nine years, we have carried this vision. You have seen us go to the field, risking our lives. For over nine years, you have been the number one beneficiary of my so-called immoral and criminal path. I used that money to support you in school; I used that money to clothe you, and I used that money to feed you. I got you posted to Lagos. I got you posted to that bank. Now, you feel you could just come up with the flimsy excuse of being well paid to suggest the unthinkable."

"Bold!"

"Don't call me that! What's come over you? Do you think I would just abandon this project like that; abandon my friends with whom I have gone through thick and thin? Do you really want me to abandon this mission of vengeance? Are you asking me to abandon the warmth of the rising sun that I see on the horizon of my chosen path? I will not abandon this long-held vision. It is a vision I have held onto very tenaciously.

"My grouse is with the bigger thieves in high places. My real grievances are targeted at those walking along the corridors of power. I am not in the military, so I cannot successfully plan and overthrow a government. Again, I'd say it at the risk of continued repetition, that these same people are the owners of most of the banks operating in this country. We only wish to recover from them some of the money they have stolen from us. And you of all people, shall not be a cog in the wheel of progress," he said with a note of finality.

That was enough warning for Eneobong. She did not need some tutelage on the scope or magnitude of Amos's readiness and capability to inflict injury. She knew he had spoken his mind, and that the best option for her now was not to argue any further with him. On request, therefore, Eneobong furnished Amos with a detailed graphic illustration of the bank's physical internal outlay: the position of the branch manager's office; the strong room; the cash manager's office; and every other detail necessary for a successful raid.

Their first bank robbery was a total hit - a complete success story for the gang. Security operatives manning the bank were totally caught unawares. When they eventually awoke from their slumber, and seeing the superior weapons being brandished by the marauders, wisdom instructed them not to resist, but to totally co-operate with the robbers. The robbers, dressed in pure military uniforms, had invaded the bank and cordoned off the street. Bank customers and passers-by initially mistook them for security men on special assignment. Only security personnel working with the bank knew that there was fire on the mountain. These security men were disarmed and used as tools for a more effective operation.

The invading team were eleven, each possessing two firearms, and having their faces masked. Besides the eight operational members, the Hawk, Adamu Musa and Njoku Nwite, a police corporal converted to the cause of robbery, all joined this all-important debut. Nike Olumoren was the only lady among them. Four of them manned the immediate frontage of the bank building, with eyes as sharp as a cats', moving to and fro, searching to detect any funny movement. The other seven held the entire bank staff and customers hostage.

As soon as they gained entrance into the bank, they ordered everybody to surrender their mobile phones and lie down, warning that any head lifted up as long as the operation lasted was in danger of being severed from its body. Within thirty minutes, they had completely emptied the bank vault, carting away with them monies totalling over five hundred and seventy-five million naira in local and foreign currencies.

That evening at Princess Sleek restaurant, the entire team found time to relax and celebrate their successful outing. There also, they shared the proceeds on paper, allocating some money to every member of the gang, including those who did not physically participate in the operation, as they thought fit to do. However, Boldface warned that they must all try to maintain their normal lifestyles for some months. He advised that nobody should be in a hurry to acquire property and movable assets worth much money. Part of the proceeds from that operation was earmarked for the purchase of more sophisticated weapons in preparation for future operations.

Soon enough, every one of them opened a business, using it as a front while seeking quicker money from their normal enterprise. Their lifestyles gradually began to change. In their various neighbourhoods, each cut the picture of a saintly person. They were never found wanting whenever philanthropic duties called. They had retained the services of Dr Akinfenwa Olona, who also became the personal physician to most of them. Every quarter, they raided a bank, though not without careful homework.

However, after months of planning to carry out a major raid anticipated to be a potential jackpot, the long arm of the law caught up with them. They had almost successfully raided Shehu Muktar's branch of Gold Bank before they ran out of luck. Everything seemed to be going well for them until two bullion vans and a truckload of combined security personnel arrived. This team was made up of soldiers and Mobile Policemen. At first, robbers keeping watch at the gate were rather confused, mentally overwhelmed by the rather large number of soldiers. Before they could summon up the courage to open fire on the soldiers, the soldiers had rounded them up.

They eventually surrendered and gave up their weapons. Meanwhile, Boldface and the others were oblivious of the new turn of events with their colleagues. As soon as they trooped out, burdened with heavy bags of banknotes, and brandishing their arms, those soldiers who had taken up strategic positions, swooped on them, shooting some in the legs. It was also too late for the gang to fight back. Like weaklings, they gave up without resistance, without a fight.

The soldiers, who on their part seemed to interpret the robbers' inability to fight back as the language of non-resistance, gently led the robbers into the waiting military truck and drove them to Obalende police station. Accordingly, they were handed over to the police. It was during interrogation that some of them began to sing. As a result, other members of the team were discreetly picked up, one after the other, with the hope that a major battle had been won against armed robbery. The police top brass, therefore, decided to use this as a publicity stunt, not only to prove their effectiveness but also as a warning signal to criminals that the police are ever ready for them.

Lightning Source UK Ltd.
Milton Keynes UK
UKHW021426060720
366103UK00008B/213